NAPOLEON HILL'S TIMELESS THOUGHTS FOR TODAY

NAPOLEON HILL'S TIMELESS THOUGHTS FOR TODAY

Napoleon Hill AND
Judith Williamson

An Approved Publication of The Napoleon Hill Foundation

MEDIA

MEDIA
Published 2019 by Gildan Media LLC
aka G&D Media
www.GandDmedia.com

Front Cover design by David Rheinhardt of Pyrographx

Interior design by Meghan Day Healey of Story Horse, LLC

Library of Congress Cataloging-in-Publication Data is available upon request

ISBN: 978-1-7225-0111-2

10 9 8 7 6 5 4 3 2 1

CONTENTS

INTRODUCTION

Napoleon Hill was born in the rugged mountains of Southwest Virginia in 1883. Nothing in his early background would give any inclination that he would spend a lifetime of studying and writing as to why some people are successful and others are not.

Hill would not remain an uneducated youth with little apparent desire to rise above the degrading poverty that engulfed most of the mountain people. Living in a very remote world with limited access to the fast changing world, life was very difficult.

Hill's mother died when he was ten years old and one year later his father married a young widow who brought many good qualities into the family. Hill's stepmother was educated, the daughter of a physician and the widow of a school principal. At once she began to encourage young Napoleon to better himself at a critical stage in his life.

Martha Banner Hill, the stepmother came into young Hill's life when he was in need of direction. The eleven year old was seen by his stepmother as a bright energetic boy with unlimited possibilities. Napoleon's stepmother was an inspiration to him during his lifetime. It was the new Mrs. Hill that helped him acquire a typewriter at age thirteen and told him that he would be known throughout the state of Virginia.

Hill became a prolific reader and writer. Today, nearly forty years after Napoleon Hill's death, his books continue to be best sellers around the world.

In this book you are getting the benefit of some of Dr. Napoleon Hill's best thoughts but you are also getting writings from Judith Williamson who for many years has been the director of the Napoleon Hill World Learning Center located at Purdue University Calumet Campus in Hammond, Indiana. Ms. Williamson is not only a student of Dr. Hill's philosophy but has taught the material at Purdue University as credit and non-credit courses. The author has lectured and conducted seminars for diverse groups in many parts of the world. She has taught Hill's classes in grade school, high school, college, corporations, and correctional institutions. The *Actions for Success* are taken directly from her professional experiences.

Napoleon Hill's Timeless Thoughts for Today is written so you do not have to read the book from beginning to end to get inspirational insight. Instead, you can select sections that appeal to you and enjoy the immediate applications in your own journey to success.

Don Green
Executive Director
Napoleon Hill Foundation

Achievement

"It seems hardly possible that things could have taken such a change for the better in so short a time. Everything is going in my favor just as strongly as it was going against me for the past couple of years or so. It is all too strange to understand, so I do not try to understand it. I just accept it and let the matter go at that."

Letter written by Napoleon Hill on May 14, 1925 to Mrs. Florence Hill from Cleveland, Ohio.

All individual achievements are the result of a motive or a combination of motives. The ten basic motives which inspire all voluntary action are:

1. The desire for self-preservation
2. The emotion of love
3. The emotion of fear
4. The emotion of sex
5. The desire for life after death
6. The desire for freedom of body and mind
7. The desire for revenge
8. The emotion of hate
9. The desire for self-expression and recognition
10. The desire for material gain

Source: *PMA Science of Success*. 1983. Pg. 15.

ACHIEVEMENT

Where will you be ten years from now
if you keep on going the way you are going?
—NAPOLEON HILL

Chart Your Course

Many people fail to realize that big success is the result of little successes achieved, often over a very long period of time. Truly successful people are long-term thinkers. They know that they must build upon each achievement and constantly learn new and better ways of doing things. A regular review of your progress is an essential part of goal-setting. A goal is little more than a wish unless it has a timetable for completion. Make sure your plan for your life includes short, medium, and long-term goals. Revise your goals as circumstances dictate, check them off when they are completed, and set new and bigger goals for yourself as you grow. And take time to reflect often to make sure you are on the right course—for you.

Today's action for success:

Be spontaneous. Create a life plan that lists your 1, 3, 5, and 7 year goals. Shakespeare states that there are seven stages of man's life. Perhaps you can review your life up until now, analyze what stages you have lived, and prepare for the next ones by creating goal sheets. It has also been stated that man changes every seven years. When you look at your life in 7 year increments, possibly you can begin to forecast where you want to be when you begin the next stage of development.

ACHIEVEMENT

Don't be afraid to aim high when choosing your life's goal, for no matter how high you aim, your achievements may fall below it.
—NAPOLEON HILL

Set Sail for Your Horizon

Many businesses today advocate "continuous improvement" as part of their quality programs. They have realized that to remain competitive in today's global economy they must constantly strive to improve every aspect of the business, otherwise they will be overtaken by the competition. The same ethic applies to individuals. All of life is a continuous learning experience. Every success and every temporary setback only serve to prepare you for the time when you will eventually prevail. Your short and medium term goals should be realistic and achievable, but your long-term goals should always far exceed your present capabilities. As the Roman poet Virgil said, "Fortune sides with him who dares."

Today's action for success:

Why not direct your thoughts to continuous, personal improvement? Look at yourself physically, socially, mentally, physically, and emotionally and prepare a self-improvement program for each area. As you decide upon your goals, you may be required to do some reading in order to better acquaint yourself with what direction you want to take. Try something new in each area. That's the beginning of true personal growth.

ACHIEVEMENT

A rudderless ship and a purposeless person
are eventually stranded on desert sand.
–NAPOLEON HILL

Condition Yourself for Success

The goals you set for yourself—like the rudder of a ship—will guide you toward your destination, and without them, like a ship without a rudder, you'll find it impossible to stay the course.

Make goal-setting a habit in your life. If you sometimes have trouble staying focused, set small, attainable goals and stick with the job until it's done. Examples might include finding a faster, more efficient way to do a routine job. Or taking the most difficult jobs first when you have the most energy and your concentration is at its highest level. Save the easiest jobs for last. A few small successes will inevitably lead to bigger achievements.

Today's action for success:

Rome wasn't built in a day and neither are you. Achievement begins with planning what you want to accomplish. You can dream reality into existence. Just be patient with yourself, explore your dreams, cultivate your imagination, and nurture your goals. When you are ready, you can then begin to create the framework that will align your dreams with the here and now. So, you have permission to dream and to enjoy it.

ACHIEVEMENT

By all means tell the world how good you are—but . . .
—NAPOLEON HILL

Action First, Credit Later

You should let others know of your achievements, with these provisions: Do it with your actions first and make sure you share the credit with others who helped you along the way. A fundamental principle of leadership that has not changed over the centuries is: Share the credit for success with others, but take the blame for failures alone.

Today's action for success:

This one simple leadership principle is worth its weight in the value you will receive when you use it with sincerity. Never underestimate the power of sharing the glory. Glory shared is not divided, but grows exponentially like a candle flame used to ignite a host of candles. The original candle is never diminished but yet the light expands. You can still be the original candle, but share the limelight!

ACHIEVEMENT

Watch the one ahead of you, and you'll learn why he is ahead.
Then emulate him.
—NAPOLEON HILL

Select a Pacesetter

One of the surest ways to achieve success is to observe the actions of successful people, determine what principles they regularly employ, and then use them yourself. The principles of success, as Andrew Carnegie said, are definite, they are real, and they can be learned by anyone willing to take the time to study and apply them. If you are truly observant, you will find that you can learn something from almost everyone you meet. And it isn't even necessary that you know them. You may choose great people who are no longer alive. The important thing is to study their lives, and then learn and apply in your own life the specific principles these people used to achieve greatness.

Today's action for success:

Napoleon Hill's Ship of Success is a good metaphor for your ongoing development. When you look at it thoughtfully, you can determine which success principles you are using and which you are not. You can continue to use only a few, or you can decide to incorporate more into your success toolkit. It's been said that when the only tool that you have is a hammer, everything looks as if it needs hammering. Refine your toolkit by incorporating the 17 principles, and remember to use each one. You will notice the difference in your handiwork.

ACHIEVEMENT

If you want a job done promptly and well, get a busy person to do it. The idle one knows too many substitutes and shortcuts.
—NAPOLEON HILL

Get a Deadline

Most of us will never know our true capacity for achievement because we never challenge ourselves to perform at our best every day. This truism becomes apparent when you are presented with an opportunity that really interests you. No matter how busy you may be, somehow you will find the time to pursue it. Conversely, duties that have little appeal for you are easily postponed and eventually forgotten.

Busy people are not procrastinators. They know that life, as John David Wright once observed about business, "is like riding a bicycle. Either you keep moving, or you fall down." The most effective people have a sense of urgency. They set deadlines and force themselves to establish priorities. Even if your activities don't usually require strict deadlines, set them for yourself. You will be amazed at how much you can accomplish in a short time—if that's all the time you have.

Today's action for success:

Think how much you could accomplish if you did only one thing each day that you dislike doing. That adds up to 30 or 31 monthly items that have been checked off your to-do list! This may sound like a game, and it can be seen as such. Regardless of how you look at it, it works and soon you will discover that just by doing the thing first that you dislike most on your list, the rest of the day is liberated! Now go ahead, and do the thing you dread doing the most!

ACHIEVEMENT

Never mind what others didn't do.
It's what you do that counts.
—NAPOLEON HILL

Hold Only You Accountable

If you depend upon others for your success, you are doomed to a life of failure and despair. It is a sad fact of life that few people consistently deliver what they promise. Instead of lamenting what someone else should have done to help you, focus on what you can do to help yourself. The best plan of action is one that provides opportunities for others to benefit if they wish to work with you toward the accomplishment of your goals but that does not depend upon these people for success.

Today's action for success:

I am the boss of me! Know this for a fact and then direct your intentions toward your success. The key here is to know that you alone are accountable and responsible for your outcome—no one else. Sometimes people spend a lifetime learning this lesson. But when you discover that you can give yourself permission to head up your own life, appoint yourself CEO, and grab the reins. Your personal success will follow. Giddyup!

ACHIEVEMENT

Most misfortunes are the result of misused time.
—NAPOLEON HILL

Watch the Clock

The only luck in the world is the luck you create for yourself. Only in the casino are the odds in favor of the house. In real life, the odds always favor those who use their time wisely to pursue their goals constructively, to fill every day with a full measure of honest work. Bad luck befalls those who waste time and mental energy hoping for the big break that will propel them to greatness. We all have the same twenty-four hours available to us in each day. Most of us spend eight hours working and eight hours sleeping. What you do with the remaining eight hours will have a tremendous influence on the level of success you achieve in your life.

Today's action for success:

For a month, keep a record of how you use your eight daily hours that are not spent working or sleeping. Notice how much time you give to leisure, to socialization, to recreation, to physical activity, to study, to spiritual growth, to worry, and to your future goals. At the end of the month, tally up the time spent and create a pie chart that indicates percentages of time spent—i.e., the slices of the pie. Now, view the chart and ask yourself if the time you are spending is propelling you in the direction you wish to go. If not, reevaluate your time and reallocate it to the direction that you want to focus on in the future. Make sure your time is well spent and not wasted.

ACHIEVEMENT

When you close the door of your mind to negative thoughts, the door of opportunity opens to you.
—NAPOLEON HILL

Answer the Door

It is the nature of opportunity that it simply refuses to attach itself to negative thinkers. Negative minds cannot conceive exciting new business opportunities, invent innovative new products, solve difficult problems, or create beautiful music or works of art. All of these activities require a positive belief in yourself and your abilities. When you approach every challenge with a Positive Mental Attitude, you will always discover opportunities that others have overlooked. Relish your achievements and recall them when the going gets tough. Take comfort in the knowledge that you have succeeded in the past and you can do it again. You can do it if you think you can!

Today's action for success:

Spend a few hours in a good bookstore browsing the shelves. Go to sections that you would normally not visit and select two or three books that interest you, but are currently out of your reading area. Commit to reading these books, if only a chapter every day or two until you complete them. Ask yourself, what new thoughts were generated because of this new information? Sometimes, imagination is ignited from an outside source. When you open up freely to receive information from multiple sources, your Positive Mental Attitude goes on active duty and you become the recipient of good things to follow. Just remember to show up for muster!

ACHIEVEMENT

You are more apt to "rust" out your brain from disuse than you are to wear it out from use.
—NAPOLEON HILL

Life-long Learner

Unlike a mechanical device that eventually wears out and must be replaced if it is used continually and consistently, the mind grows only stronger when it is active. The more you exercise and stretch your brain, the more proficient it becomes. Disuse, however, will have the same effect upon your mind as it will upon a machine. The most intricate, most powerful machine in the world and the greatest minds will rust away unless they are used.

Unless you manage your schedule to permit time for study and learning, it is easy to yield to the temptation to spend your free time in thoughtless, mind-numbing, escapist pastimes. Relaxation is important, but so is gaining new knowledge. Make sure your daily schedule includes an allotment of time for both.

Today's action for success:

Life-long learners enjoy life more. They develop multiple interests and talents. They are drawn to learning because they reap benefits from what they have learned before and expect to continue to do so with each new learning experience. Learning does not end upon graduation. Graduation is simply a going forth with the anticipation of actively doing things in the outside world. Renew and refresh your learning experience if you have not remained current. Boredom will never show up on your doorstep as long as you have something to learn. When the "Back to School" sales are on, go shopping and fill up your book bag with pens, pencils, paper, markers, etc. You will be inspired to begin something new.

ACHIEVEMENT

Some people are never free from troubles, mainly because they keep their minds attuned to worry. The mind attracts what it dwells on.
—NAPOLEON HILL

Eliminate the Negative

Worry serves no useful purpose and can have a serious adverse effect upon your mental as well as your physical health. Charles Mayo, who with his brother William founded the famous Mayo Clinic in Rochester, Minnesota, said, "I have never known a man who died from overwork, but many who died from doubt."

Because worry is directed at some vague, uncertain threat, it is difficult to deal with it logically. The best way to get rid of your worries is to take positive action to eliminate their source. When you develop a plan for dealing constructively with problems and get to work implementing your plan, you will no longer be troubled by worries. Negative thoughts always yield the right of way to a determined person in pursuit of a positive plan of action.

Today's action for success:

Here is an idea on how to eliminate your worries. Write your individual worries on single pieces of paper. Look them over, and consider each one. Next, using a small candle safely placed on a fireproof surface, hold each worry with tweezers and burn it saying "Worry Be Gone!" This sends a message to your subconscious mind that underscores your desire to be once and for all through with these worries. Finally, on the same number of slips of papers, write out a positive belief that now will replace the worry. These can be affirmations that you need when your worry begins to come back to stalk you.

ACHIEVEMENT

The best job goes to the one who can get it done without passing the buck or coming back with alibis.
—NAPOLEON HILL

The Buck Stop

We often discover that people we view as "overnight successes" have in fact labored for years in obscurity before they were finally recognized and rewarded for their contributions. Success is a cumulative effort; the journey to the top in any field is usually long and requires careful planning.

If you want to climb the first rung on the ladder of success, you must always take the initiative to get the job done, even when you find it less than challenging or even unpleasant. Eventually, you'll earn your reward. You will become the boss, the leader, because you have developed the habit of taking the initiative to get the job done. You will get the best jobs because you've proven that you are dependable by accepting responsibility for your actions and your future.

Today's action for success:

Success is a cumulative effort. This is a statement worth pondering. What may seem easy or like instantaneous success usually isn't. By taking action toward achievement oriented tasks people prepare their foundation for success over the years. Nothing happens overnight, and when it does it usually has no substance. Once you decide upon your definite major purpose, you can then begin to work on laying the foundation, building the structure, installing the drywall, plumbing, electrical work, etc., before you begin to furnish the rooms. One step at a time undertaken daily results in a journey of a thousand miles that begins with one step.

ACHIEVEMENT

Your progress in life begins in your own mind
and ends in the same place.
—NAPOLEON HILL

Progress Through Discipline

Every great accomplishment began with the germ of an idea in the mind of a great person, then was shaped for practical usefulness and finally transformed into reality. Make your mind a fertile ground for ideas through constant study and learning, and condition through constant practice to discipline yourself to follow through on your good ideas. The most brilliant concept in the world is only a dream unless you take action. Even a mediocre idea that is put into practice is far more valuable than a flash of genius that languishes in a fallow, undisciplined mind.

Today's action for success:

To be a success, you must have discipline. Discipline separates the dreamers from the doers, the wannabees from the winners. Discipline creates the structure, the container for your thoughts to take shape and progress toward an outcome. Without discipline your dreams remain an amorphous mass that never solidify into success. How are you disciplining yourself for your advancement?

ACHIEVEMENT

If you work as hard at the task you desire to do
as the task you must do, you will go places.
—NAPOLEON HILL

Are you ready?

It's been said that you should always work at two jobs simultaneously: the one you have and the one you desire. When you work as hard at the task you want to do as the task you must do, you are preparing yourself for the future. You are learning skills that will enable you to grow beyond your present position and into your boss's job and your boss's boss's job. When the time comes, you'll be ready.

When you've mastered one task, don't rest on your laurels. Instead, begin immediately to think about the future, about how you can improve what you're doing now, and what you can learn that will allow you to progress in the future. Ours is a knowledge-based economy in which intellectual property is worth far more than physical goods. To succeed today requires continuous learning; staying current in your field means a lifetime of study in our fast-paced world.

Today's action for success:

Stay the course! Do the thing and you shall have the power! Do it now! Don't give up the ship! All of these are commands focused on action. Action produces results. You can't command a ship sitting on shore, drive a tank from a merry-go-round, achieve success watching television 24/7. You get the idea. Now, prepare yourself for your future success by emulating those who have already achieved what you desire. The roadmap is there. Just follow it.

ACHIEVEMENT

Remember, your mental limitations are of your own making.
—NAPOLEON HILL

What's Your Limit?

For years, athletes attempted to run a mile in four minutes but it seemed to be a barrier that no one could overcome. Then on May 6, 1954, a British runner named Roger Gilbert Bannister ran a mile in 3:59.4 minutes to establish a world record. Soon afterward, other runners broke Bannister's record. Too often, we accept conventional wisdom as fact. Make sure you set your goals high enough. Don't settle for less because of limitations you place upon yourself. Most of us never really reach the level of achievement of which we are capable because we don't challenge ourselves to do so. Perhaps Robert Browning said it best: "A man's reach should exceed his grasp, or what's a heaven for?"

Today's action for success:

Ask yourself why your reach should exceed your grasp? Why dare to dream big? Are you afraid to expect the best for yourself? Why? What holds you back? What one dream would you pursue if you knew you could measure up? Now, sit back and dream big—just for once. Let your imagination carry you to stellar heights. Go right past the moon and reach for the stars. When you arrive, let your dream touch your senses—see, hear, taste, smell and touch what it will be like. Now, quickly write it down, date it, reread it, and secure it. Daily, as in a ritual, reread what you have written and in a daily diary record how inch by inch you are advancing toward this dream.

Adversity

"I have stood by this Law of Success lecture, and my fifteen points for more than seven years. At times they only seemed to mock me, when I was talking of success to others while my own family suffered for the necessities. I have not just known why I did this. At times I wondered as you have done, if I would not have been better off to have forgotten it all and have gone back to some little job as bookkeeper, where I could have earned at least a modest living. BUT, there was something that would not let me do it. I have stood my grounds, suffered, been disappointed, and given disappointment to others, all because I could not do otherwise. I was simply helpless in the matter. If it turns out all right, then I will take no credit, for I would have changed my course a dozen times in the last six or seven years, if I COULD HAVE DONE SO."

Letter written by Napoleon Hill on 7/13/1925 to Mrs. Florence Hill from Massillon, Ohio.

ADVERSITY

Great Achievement is born out of struggle.
–NAPOLEON HILL

Strength through Weakness

"Our strength grows out of our weakness," said Ralph Waldo Emerson. "Not until we are pricked and stung and sorely shot at, awakens the indignation which arms itself with secret forces." Strife and struggle can inspire you to overcome adversity and to propel yourself to real achievement. View every struggle as an opportunity for personal growth. It is the struggle itself, not the result that builds character. If you know you are right, stay the course even though the whole world seems to be against you and everyone you know questions your judgment. When you prevail—and you eventually will if you stick to the job—they will all tell you that they knew all along you could do it.

Today's action for success:

Take a piece of loose leaf paper. Draw a line down the middle. On top of the left hand column write "weaknesses." On top of the right hand column write "strengths." Now, without much conscious thought, list twenty of your weaknesses in three to five minutes. Next, on the right hand side, write down a strength or a potential strength that could grow out of this weakness. Remember the seed you plant determines the harvest that you will get. Even seeds of adversity will mature into seeds of success if you know how to plant and nurture them. Why not uncover some of your hidden talents today?

ADVERSITY

Don't look to the stars for the cause of your misfortunes.
Look to yourself to get better results.
—NAPOLEON HILL

You Control Your Destiny

There are many things you cannot control, but you can control the only things that really matter: your mind and your attitude. External forces have very little to do with success. Those who program themselves for success find a way to succeed even in the most difficult of circumstances. Solutions to most problems come from one source and one source alone: yourself.

Living life to the fullest is a lot like shooting the rapids in a rubber raft. Once you've made the commitment, it's difficult to change your mind, turn around, and paddle upstream to placid waters. But it's the excitement and adventure that make it all worthwhile. If you never make the attempt, you may never know the depths of despair, but neither will you experience the exhilaration of success.

Today's action for success:

Decide to live life to the fullest. Accept the challenge of "I dare you" and become what only you can dream. I dare you to take a trip overseas! I dare you to take a class on self-improvement and not only read the material, but do the exercises preparatory to the outcomes. I dare you to turn an enemy into a friend. And, this day I dare you to do an unselfish act of service for no visible compensation. And, by the way, "Do it now!"

ADVERSITY

The person who complains that he or she never had a chance probably hasn't the courage to take a chance.
—NAPOLEON HILL

The Courage to Take a Chance

Thomas Edison once observed that the reason most folks don't recognize opportunity when it comes along is that it is often dressed in coveralls and looks like work. Often opportunity involves a great deal of work and a willingness to take a chance on something, the outcome of which may be uncertain.

Eventually you reach a point when you must either accept an opportunity with all of its unknowns or else turn your back on it. No one can tell you when you have reached that point; you alone know when it's time to make your move, to have the courage to take a chance.

Today's action for success:

Chances not taken are missed opportunities forever. When opportunity knocks and finds no one home you have just missed your fairy godmother of success. Dr. Hill tells us to act immediately when the thought or opportunity hits us. If we take time to consider the proposal, oftentimes someone else has tuned into the thought, accepted the challenge, and is on the success beam before you even arrive home to answer the door. Today, when opportunity knocks, open the door and shake hands with success! Have the courage to accept the opportunity and make it work for you.

ADVERSITY

No one can keep you down but yourself.
—NAPOLEON HILL

Friend or Foe?

Have you ever felt that sometimes you are your own worst enemy? We all have moments when, no matter how hard we try, things just don't seem to work out right, when everything goes wrong, and we have no one to blame but ourselves. But, just as you may sometimes be your own worst enemy, you can also be your own best friend. The transition usually occurs when you realize that the only person on earth who can determine your failure or success is you yourself.

You may discover your best friend when you develop the maturity and strength of character to accept yourself for the person you are and to take the actions necessary to become the person you wish to be. When you analyze yourself objectively, you can begin to build upon your strengths and compensate for your weaknesses. When you do, you will realize that the only person who stands in the way of your success is you.

Today's action for success:

It's a known technique that if you desire a characteristic, the best way to acquire it is to act as if you already possess it. Want to be a leader in your field? Ask yourself how leaders in your line of work behave and then do likewise. Prepare yourself for the position as if it were already yours. This works beyond the job setting as well. Want more friends? Watch how people with many friends behave and next follow their example. When considering certain careers, review rating scales that indicate superior performance for these professionals. Make it your choice to then follow actively in their footsteps. Remember, success steps taken one at a time soon accumulate into the destination of your choice.

ADVERSITY

It isn't defeat, but rather your mental attitude
toward it, that whips you.
—NAPOLEON HILL

Defeat—The Imposter

There are many things in life that you cannot control, but you can always control your attitude toward them. Defeat is never permanent unless you allow it to be so. When you have a positive attitude, you will recognize failure for the impostor that it is and realize that it is really a learning experience, a valuable lesson that will help you succeed with the next attempt.

Ask yourself: What could I have done differently that would have altered the outcome? What can I do in the future to minimize problems and mistakes? What did I learn from this experience that I can put to good use next time? If you approach obstacles and setbacks with a positive attitude, you will be surprised how quickly you can turn defeat into victory.

Today's action for success:

It's been said that failure isn't failure until you accept it as such. How many times have you allowed someone in your life to determine what you can or cannot do? By giving away your locus of control, you are harming your self-confidence and destroying your personal power. Today, stop allowing others to define your life. Make it your mission to determine what it is you want to do. If you have a desire to do something, the desire alone predetermines your capability to succeed at it. Persistence is the key to positive outcomes. You may not be able, at first, to do it as quickly or as flawlessly as someone who has been at it longer, but be guaranteed that when you put in the time you will reap results in the near future. Remember an oak tree is just a little acorn that stood its ground.

ADVERSITY

> Who told you it couldn't be done, and what great achievements has he performed that qualified him to set up limitations for you?
>
> —NAPOLEON HILL

Value of Free Advice

You will find as you go through life that those who give advice most freely are precisely the individuals who are least qualified to do so. Busy, successful people don't have an interest in telling you how to live your life. They are busy living their own. Failures or mediocre people have all the time in the world. They also delight in seeing you fail, and are quick to say "I told you so" when you experience a temporary setback.

If someone tells you that what you are attempting to achieve is impossible or not worth the effort, take a close look at them and what they have accomplished with their lives. The chances are good that you will find they haven't done much. Successful people are optimistic people. They have the habit of success because they learned long ago to listen to themselves and not to those who would like to see them fail.

Today's action for success:

Ever hear about Dr. Hill's Invisible Counselors? These were mental guides that he put on watch for his best interests. He created them as reminders to himself to perform well in certain capacities. At times, he referred to them as Princes. For example, there was the Prince of Sound Health and his purpose was to watch over Dr. Hill's health status. This approach was much like what others do in list making or in the writing of reminder notes that are posted in certain locations. In truth, these strategies serve as alarm clocks to wake us from our slumber into reality. Otherwise, we might forget our true purpose. Who can you place on watch for your best interests? Surely, it won't be someone with negative opinions about you. Rather, put some invisible friend in charge of you who only looks out for your best interests. Then, check in with him daily to make certain your reports are always in the tip top shape.

ADVERSITY

If you don't know what you want,
don't say you never had a chance.
—NAPOLEON HILL

Winner versus Loser

The people who complain the loudest about never having an opportunity in life are usually the ones who always have a ready excuse for their failures. Nothing is ever their fault; they are victims of their heritage, their environment, insufficient education, or any number of other factors that they perceive as placing them at a disadvantage. If you look hard enough, you can always find reasons for not attempting something or not sticking with the job to the end. Successful people, though, are not excuse makers. They take responsibility for their actions, they set goals, and they assume responsibility for their achievement. Where others see despair, they see hope. They approach every situation with enthusiasm, confident in the knowledge that nothing is impossible for those who have a Positive Mental Attitude.

Today's action for success:

See life as your oyster. Step forward with a positive mental attitude. Never declare that things are working against you. Rather, step up to the plate and hit a home run because you know you can. Invalidate people's negative commentary just as you would an outdated prescription. Say cancel, cancel mentally and know for certain that it will not harm you or hold you back. No one can step inside your skin and diagnose that you are either less or more than you know yourself to be. You, and you alone, are the predictor of the outcome of your life. So, begin today by writing yourself positive prescriptions for success. Napoleon Hill believed in mental vitamins. Prescribe a daily dose of these mental vitamins for yourself and become healthy, happy and terrific day by day in every way.

ADVERSITY

It's not the epitaph on your tombstone but the record of your deeds that may perpetuate your name after death.
—NAPOLEON HILL

My Obituary

Alfred Nobel had an opportunity afforded to very few. When his brother died, the newspaper confused the two and published Alfred's obituary instead of his brother's. As he read his own obituary, Alfred realized that the world would remember him for his invention of dynamite—an instrument of destruction. It was because of that experience that he decided to fund the Nobel Prizes. Today, most of the world knows his name in connection with humankind's greatest achievements.

Good deeds live on in the minds of others. When you do a kindness for someone else, you set in motion a force for good that will remain long after you're gone.

Today's action for success:

Ask yourself what you would do for the world if you had unlimited resources to fund your dream. Write your project down on paper. Get specific. Be detailed. Make it several paragraphs. Read it aloud to yourself. Amend it. Read it aloud to someone else who will provide a listening heart. Now, even if you do not have a penny to contribute to the manifestation of the project, you have already begun by putting the written and spoken word out to the Universe. Get serious and ask yourself what preliminary steps you could take now to get this project off the ground. List ten things that you could do without funds that would advance the project forward—if only by inches. Then, do these things. Remember, thinking makes it so.

ADVERSITY

Many successful people have found opportunities
in failure and adversity that they could not recognize
in more favorable circumstances.
—NAPOLEON HILL

From Desperation to Success

Samuel Johnson once observed that the prospect of being hanged wonderfully focuses the mind. You yourself may have found that your mind seems sharpest when you are faced with the greatest difficulties. Desperation often proves you really are better than you think. But with the exception of an immediate threat to your life or health, there are few situations that require instantaneous action. When the world seems to be conspiring against you and nothing is working out right, pause for a few moments to think the situation through—then develop the most appropriate plan of action, the one that has the greatest likelihood of success.

Today's action for success:

If life has caught you hanging by your fingernails, you either have to abandon ship or drown. Many times it seems as if there is no good option, but when you creatively consider what else you might do, ideas begin to fill your head. One technique that works is to keep asking yourself the question "What next?" in response to resolving your dilemma. This prompt usually produces responses that at least give you an option for the next step that you might take. Just knowing that you have options at times can be enough of an incentive to turn the tide. "Don't give up the ship" is the slogan for the U.S. Navy, and it is a good command. Never abandon something that is meaningful to you. If you do, your life's treasure will go down with the ship.

ADVERSITY

Edison failed 10,000 times before perfecting the incandescent electrical light bulb. Don't worry if you fail once.
—NAPOLEON HILL

Obstacles into Steppingstones

Arguably America's greatest inventor, Thomas Edison had an extraordinarily positive perception of life that greatly enhanced his ability as an inventor. When others might have been hopelessly discouraged after failing thousands of times in an attempt to develop an electric light, the great Edison simply viewed each unsuccessful experiment as the elimination of a solution that wouldn't work, thereby moving him that much closer to a successful solution.

We could all take a lesson from Edison. Stories abound about inventors who quit trying and gave up too soon or miners who struck gold just a few feet beyond where someone else quit digging. There are few obstacles in life that will not succumb to consistent, sustained, intelligent, positive action. When you are discouraged after you've failed at something, remember Edison's 10,000 failures before he arrived at the solution that forever changed the world.

Today's action for success:

View failures as potential future successes and you will always come out a winner. How can we be certain that failures are not built into the great scheme of things by a Universal Intelligence that prefers that we learn life lessons from struggle? As humans, adversity touches us emotionally. It's a known fact that when we attack our definite major purpose with heightened emotions, we reach our goal more quickly due to our capacity to arouse ourselves to action. Want something done sooner than later? Get emotional about the goal and your outcome will be a function of how much head and heart you have pulled together for your ultimate victory.

ADVERSITY

Success requires no explanation;
failures must be doctored with alibis.
—NAPOLEON HILL

Blame or Fame?

The surest way to achieve acceptance in any organization or in any line of work is to be successful. Unfortunately, life doesn't work that way. No matter how carefully you study a subject, no matter how rationally you make decisions, no matter how well prepared you are, you will occasionally make mistakes. Human beings always do. The important thing is to realize that temporary setbacks are not permanent failures. Successful people recognize that we all experience temporary setbacks that require us to reevaluate our performance and take corrective action to achieve success. They know that adversity is never permanent.

Today's action for success:

Take a deep breath, sit back, take pen in hand, and on the notebook in front of you write ten things that mentally and emotionally meant something to you that you failed at in your life. With these failures staring you in the face, ask yourself for each one, what ultimately caused the failure? When we mature in wisdom and in age, we begin to understand that ultimately we are accountable for our failures and no one else. Take time to see this seed of wisdom in each of your listed failures. Now, see if you can begin to uncover a pattern, a history, a thread that weaves its way through the course of your life. If this ends up being a person other than yourself, ask yourself why you have given this person control over your life. Finally, take back the control you willingly abdicated and become once again the only boss you will ever need—the one under your own hat!

ADVERSITY

There always remains an opportunity to make a new start.
—NAPOLEON HILL

The Most Important Thing

Though it may not seem so when you first encounter a serious blow, you can never lose two of the most important assets you have. These are the power of your mind and your freedom to use it. Once you have turned them to understanding what laid you low, you can begin forming new plans. You may not have the money you once had; you may lack the allies you had cultivated. But you still have the benefit of a universe that eventually rewards honest effort, as well as gaining the experience of mistakes you will never make again.

Remember, no matter where you are now, whatever you can conceive and believe, you can achieve. Protect the most important thing you have.

Today's action for success:

When you have been dealt that fateful blow and it pierces you to the quick, right then is the time to get up and begin again—now, not tomorrow. Everything may be gone but if you can still think, you have the power to not only rebound but recover from your losses. Education, whether it is through the lessons life teaches us or formal in nature, is the only thing that cannot be taken from us. Think about it. If you're married and then divorce, your personal degrees—say a B.A. or a Ph.D.—are not split down the middle. The husband doesn't get the "B" and the wife the "A." Rather, the person who has earned the education keeps it. Knowing that, isn't it time you get busy and deposit some wisdom in your personal account? Invest in yourself. You are definitely worth it.

ADVERSITY

Most failures could have been converted into successes if someone had held on another minute or made more effort.
—NAPOLEON HILL

Don't give up the Ship!

When you have the potential for success within you, adversity and temporary defeat only help you prepare to reach great heights of success. Without adversity, you would never develop the qualities of reliability, loyalty, humility, and perseverance that are so essential to enduring success. Many people have escaped the jaws of defeat and achieved great victories because they would not allow themselves to fail. When your escape routes are all closed, you will be surprised how quickly you will find the path to success.

Today's action for success:

Are you a chef, or at least a cook? Have there been times that the new recipe you tried did not meet your culinary expectations? Did the dog or cat have a new entrée in the lunch bowl? Well, what happened next is most important. Was there a meal on the table or did you abandon cooking altogether? I think that we can safely assume that you did not throw out your pots and pans; however, you may have found a new cookbook. If we view adversity as the opposite of a recipe for success, we will begin to understand how flops can turn into successes. Maybe the ingredients were bad, maybe the oven was too hot, or maybe the measurements were off—whatever the problem, on the next opportunity we are able to make those corrections that with a little practice deliver a culinary masterpiece. Why not try your hand at something new today? Remember the old adage, "If at first you don't succeed, try, try again!"

ADVERSITY

Success attracts success and failure attracts failure because of the law of harmonious attraction.
—NAPOLEON HILL

Like Attracts Like

In physics, positives attract negatives and vice versa, but in human relationships the opposite is true. Negative people attract only other negative people, while positive thinkers attract like-minded individuals. You will find that when you begin to achieve success, more successes will follow. This is the law of harmonious attraction. When riches begin to come your way, you'll be amazed how quickly they accumulate. Train your mind to visualize yourself acquiring a specific amount of wealth or achieving a certain goal—whatever you most desire. Then use self-suggestion to persuade your subconscious mind that you can achieve your goal, and put your plan into action. When you use the tools that you have at your disposal to prepare yourself for success and visualize yourself as having already reached your objective, you can achieve any reasonable goal that you set for yourself.

Today's action for success:

Think for a moment about the organizations that you believe in and even support. There is a 100% likelihood that these organizations align with your interests, values, and beliefs. If you were not drawn to them, you would not be inclined to dedicate your time to them. In life, our thoughts, ideas, interests, values, and beliefs on an ascending scale add up to who we are. Although invisible, these are the vibrations we throw out for other people to catch. We are drawn to others and others to us because of these very real, yet invisible vibrations of thought. As you radiate these vibes, ask yourself if you are a shinning star or a death star? A roaring bonfire or a matchstick? A fragrant rose or an odiferous weed? Make a list of your personal characteristics. Then decide to look at these characteristics on a continuum ranging from 0 to 100%. How close are you to either extreme? If improvement is needed, it is for you to decide. Remember, like attracts like. What you think about you become. Doesn't it make sense to take an inventory of our personal vibes? Bottom line—who are you attracting?

ADVERSITY

Failure seems to be nature's plan for preparing us
for great responsibilities.
—NAPOLEON HILL

Achievement Preparation

If everything we attempted in life was achieved with a minimum of effort and came out exactly as planned, how little we would learn—and how boring life would be! And how arrogant we would become if we succeeded at everything we attempted. Failure allows us to develop the essential quality of humility. It is not easy—when you are the person experiencing failure—to accept it philosophically, serene in the knowledge that this is one of life's great learning experiences. But it is. Nature's ways are not always easily understood, but they are repetitive and therefore predictable. You can be absolutely certain that when you feel you are being most unfairly tested, you are being prepared for great achievement.

Today's action for success:

Have you ever been asked the question: "What would you do if you knew you couldn't fail?" Usually, we respond that we would "reach for the stars" in whatever area of life we are engaged in at the time. Napoleon Hill says: "If wishes were horses beggars would ride." This is not a disgruntled quote, but rather a truism that we should all heed. If things come too easily, then everyone would have them and these "things" would not have the importance that they do for us now. Life is made up of challenges to be mastered. Those that we cannot easily master on our first attempts take a little longer but ultimately prove more worthy. When we persist, we are saying to the Universe that we can't fail because we are unwilling to concede defeat. Just one more try, just one more inch, just one more homework assignment, can and will make the difference between victory and defeat.

Cooperation

There is always a place for the person who can create harmony in human relationships.

Friendly counsel carries more weight than unfriendly criticism. Think what I please, but be careful how I express my thoughts.

I cannot succeed and remain successful without the friendly cooperation of others.

No person can become a permanent success without taking others along with them.

The sure way to promote yourself is to help others get ahead.

A good team consists in harmonious coordination of effort more than in individual skill.

Most men will respond more freely to a request than they will to an order.

A friend is one who comes to your rescue when you are wrong as quickly as when you are right—if you have one such you are fortunate.

Never ask anyone to do anything for you that you wouldn't do for him or her if the circumstances were reversed.

Quotations by Dr. Hill

COOPERATION

A good football team relies more on harmonious coordination of effort than individual skill.
–NAPOLEON HILL

How to Score

Teamwork is a "cooperative effort by the members of a team to achieve a common goal." The key words in the definition are cooperative effort. Without the support of the entire group, no team can long endure. Football players quickly learn that no member of the team can be a star in every play. Most moments of glory are built upon a long series of plays, each won by committed, determined, bone-jarring blocking and tackling.

A winning team is one whose members recognize that when one member of the team is successful, the entire team wins. Conversely, a sure way to develop a losing formula is to create an environment in which team members compete with one another instead of the opponent. When all members give their best in every situation—whether they are carrying the ball or clearing the way for someone else—the team wins and so does each individual member of it.

Today's action for success:

You have heard the expression—There ain't no "I" in team. This is a fact worth remembering when you are accepting credit for something that was accomplished by a team. Make certain that you overlook no person who made a contribution. If you do, you may find yourself operating all alone IF and when you stand up to take credit the next time.

COOPERATION

Friction in machinery costs money. Friction in human relationships impoverishes both the spirit and the bank account.
—NAPOLEON HILL

The Holy "No"

Discord in any relationship often has unpleasant financial implications, but it is far costlier in human terms. When you are involved in a fractious relationship, physical and mental energy that could be directed toward positive achievements is dissipated needlessly, squandered upon stressful, unproductive activities. Unfortunately, whatever the cause of friction between individuals, it adversely affects each person involved.

When you find yourself in a contentious relationship, there are few acceptable alternatives. You can work out your problems or leave the team. Only you know which is the best solution for you, but if you objectively evaluate your reasons for becoming involved and find that they are still valid, your best course of action may be to swallow your pride and find a solution that is acceptable to everyone involved. If you cannot do this, perhaps it's time to get out of the partnership and find another course toward your objective.

Today's action for success:

Knowing when to participate in a group as a team player as well as knowing when to call it quits requires personal reflection and insight. Sometimes teams appeal to certain individuals but do not have the characteristics that match our own objectives. When we find ourselves misplaced, it is far better to pull up stakes and move on than to make the entire group miserable with our presence. Mismatches occur. I am sure that you can think of times when you have been in this situation. Fortunately, it's an easy one to resolve. Just say that this group does not align with your personal goals, and move on. I have heard decisions like this called the "Holy No" and I can understand why. We are being spiritually true to our own nature when we decline to participate in something that has no real purpose for us.

COOPERATION

If you cannot agree with others, you can at least refrain from quarreling with them.
—NAPOLEON HILL

Agree to Disagree Agreeably

When you are involved in a dispute with someone else, it may be the only time doing nothing is better than doing something. There's a practical reason for this: When you quarrel with others—even if you win the argument—you place a great deal of unnecessary stress upon yourself. It is impossible to maintain a Positive Mental Attitude when you allow negative emotions such as anger or hate to dominate your thoughts.

No one can upset you or make you angry unless you allow them to do so. Instead of arguing with others, try asking non threatening questions such as: "Why do you feel this way? What have I done to make you angry? What can I do to help?" You may find that the entire situation has resulted from a simple misunderstanding that can be quickly rectified. Even if problems are more serious, your positive behavior will go a long way toward helping resolve them.

Today's action for success:

Remind yourself that just because a person disagrees with you, you are not being judged as a person. When we take a position or stance, many times we allow our personalities to get in the way of our judgment. Practice removing yourself personally from the decisions you make. This takes conscious effort, but when you achieve it you eliminate much of the stress behind the decision making—both for the decisions that you make and also for the ones others make for you.

COOPERATION

Remember, it takes at least two people to carry on a quarrel.
—NAPOLEON HILL

Find a Positive Solution

It's difficult to remember in the heat of a disagreement that it takes two to quarrel. It may help to remember that no one can disagree with you while you are agreeing with them. This is not to suggest that you should compromise your principles. It is possible, however, to remain true to your beliefs while simultaneously searching for common ground that will enable you to work productively with others who may at first disagree with you.

When others are upset with you or with a situation that involves you, let them know that you understand how they feel. Examine the problem from their point of view. What is the source of the conflict? How could it be resolved in a manner that would satisfy the interests of all involved? How have you contributed to the problem? When you try to find solutions instead of attempting to affix blame, others will almost always respond in kind.

Today's action for success:

Be a solution finder not a problem fixer. If we remember to focus on the positive outcome always, we will always create positive results. Remember to adjust the focus from person to situation, and you will find that a positive resolution is much easier to achieve.

COOPERATION

Friendly cooperation is never any part of the devil's work.
He is working on the other side.
—NAPOLEON HILL

Take Control

The noblest human relationships are those that have been formed in a spirit of cooperation and harmony. Cooperation, in many ways, is the physical manifestation of your care and concern for your fellow man. When you work with others in a spirit of friendly cooperation, you are conducting yourself according to the founding principles of most religions and all successful societies. Everyone occasionally feels pangs of jealousy or envy, usually accompanied by the urge to cause problems or difficulty for those we dislike. Truly successful people have learned to restrain such urges. They know that if they concentrate upon their own objectives and help others along the way, they will eventually reach their goals. It isn't easy to always be a friendly, cooperative person, but in the end you will find that it is worth the effort.

Today's action for success:

By controlling our temper we control our outcome. Ever fly off the handle at someone? Did you gain any ground by doing so? I think not. By losing control you demonstrated that you cannot conduct yourself in the best manner. Maybe you had your say, but did you get your way? Solving a problem involves cooperation and discussion, not pettiness and loud voices. Before you blow off, think who is really getting the last word.

COOPERATION

All enduring success is founded upon
harmonious human relationships.
—NAPOLEON HILL

Perfect Harmony

A Master Mind alliance involves two or more people working together in perfect harmony toward the attainment of a common purpose. Such a partnership creates a superpower that enables each of its members to do far more than either would have been able to achieve separately. Choose your Master Mind partners carefully. Align yourself with people whose strengths complement yours. If you are a right brain person, for example, a logically-driven left brain person may be a perfect counterbalance to your creative bent. Above all, choose to associate only with people who share your positive values and your commitment to similar levels of achievement.

Today's action for success:

The key to a successful Mastermind Alliance is that the members work together in perfect harmony. Each member must make a unique contribution to the alliance and thereby the entire group benefits. Why not try your hand a creating a mastermind alliance to achieve a particular goal? Usually, the fewer the number of members the better, but you can decide on how many members you need based upon the scope of your goal. Remember also, that whatever compensation is given it must be given equally. Equal does not mean the same. Equal means whatever is determined to be equal in the mind of the recipient. Goals tackled by a mastermind alliance can be manifested quickly. There is magic in numbers.

COOPERATION

If you appreciate the kindness shown you by others,
say it with actions as well as words.
—NAPOLEON HILL

Sow a Deed

The people who enjoy the greatest financial and personal success in life are those who build lasting relationships—with business associates, friends, co-workers, and others. They take the time and trouble to stay in touch, and they make sure that when someone does a good deed for them, they respond in kind. Build your network of personal and professional friends by taking the initiative and being a friend.

Today's action for success:

Make a list of ways to build friendships. These things do not have to be expensive or even time consuming. By doing small things that show you care you are creating lifelong relationships a deed at a time. Give it a try. Go beyond what you would normally do today in remembering a friend. Send an e-card, make a phone call, write a note, deliver a little gift, bake a dessert, stop for coffee, or visit a museum for starters. When you make time for friends, they always blossom and so do you.

COOPERATION

Willing cooperation produces enduring power,
while forced cooperation ends in failure.
—NAPOLEON HILL

The Golden Rule

No civilization based upon the unjust treatment of its people has ever endured. A tyrant may force the cooperation of others for a time, but that power is never sustained. Only when people are accorded the respect they deserve do they willingly create and maintain successful organizations and societies. When you build a company or an organization based on fairness and justice for every member, you have built a power that will long endure.

The best way to secure the commitment and unending cooperation of others is through the simple application of the Golden Rule. It is the most successful and long-lasting management theory ever developed. When you treat others as you would like to be treated were you in their situation, you will inspire loyalty and enthusiastic cooperation. Set high standards for yourself and others, treat them well, let them do their jobs, and they will perform miracles for you.

Today's action for success:

It may be trite, old, and not newsworthy, but the Golden Rule is by far the best method of dealing with people throughout your lifetime. By treating others as you would like to be treated, you model the behavior you are seeking as well as creating a circle of good feelings. Remember to ask yourself how you would feel about the treatment you are extending to others. If the answer is not positive, revisit your actions and improve upon them. Why wait until someone says that you hurt them? Think the Golden Rule before you act, and then act. Positive outcomes will follow.

COOPERATION

No one can succeed and remain successful
without the friendly cooperation of others.
—NAPOLEON HILL

Give to Get

In today's interdependent society, it is virtually impossible in any business, profession, or occupation for an individual to achieve great heights of success without the help of others. The best way to get friendly cooperation is to give it. When you make it a practice to encourage others and to help them advance in their careers whenever possible, most will reciprocate when you need their help. Give generously, and you will benefit in kind.

Today's action for success:

When you give, you receive more. Not only do you enjoy the gift of giving, but you experience the gift of knowing that you brightened someone else's day. This feeling warms us as we anticipate the reception our gift is going to receive, gladdens us when our gift is accepted, and delights us afterwards as we reflect on the happiness we took part in creating. So much is gained from so little. Why would anyone not enjoy being a giver?

COOPERATION

Cooperation must start at the head of a department
if it is expected at the other end.
The same is true for efficiency.
—NAPOLEON HILL

Compete with Yourself

In most large organizations, the amount of time and energy that is squandered in interdepartmental rivalry is enormous. Managers who compete with others inside the company waste valuable resources that should be directed at fulfilling the company's mission to serve its customers better. Worse, a negative, internal focus can cause the company to miss opportunities, the full effect of which may not be realized for months or even years. Whether you are the head of the department or the newest worker on the staff, you can help your company immeasurably by refusing to become embroiled in internal strife. Compete with yourself to do the best job you can do instead of competing with others.

Today's action for success:

The only person you should compete with is yourself. Exceed your last best performance. Challenge yourself daily to do better than you have done before. Set the goal higher, and each time raise your standard. The only person who needs know this is you. When you reach the bar, award yourself with an even higher goal.

COOPERATION

Friendly cooperation always pays off because this sort of teamwork creates a positive mental attitude, which does not recognize obstacles.
—NAPOLEON HILL

Leader of Many

In any organized endeavor, obstacles are going to occur. Sometimes they appear in the form of technical problems; sometimes they are disputes between members of the team over which course is best to follow. If you have set an example of initiative and open communication, you will find that your team has the mental and spiritual resources to overcome these kinds of struggles.

A group of people who trust their leader and one another don't waste energy jockeying for prestige. They know that they will all benefit from a solution, and they are motivated to find it by sharing the knowledge and ideas. From these many parts a skilled leader can create the necessary solution, but only if a spirit of friendliness and honesty prevails.

Today's action for success:

In the Marine Corp there is a saying: "Leader of one, leader of many, if you can't lead one you can't lead any!" How true this is. We must have the first victory over ourselves before we can attempt to influence others in any direction. A leader must be worthy of followers. People only respect those who do what they say they will do. Be a leader who motivates people to become their best. When you have their best interests at heart, they have your best interest at heart too.

COOPERATION

Remember that no one can hurt your feelings
without your cooperation and willingness.
—NAPOLEON HILL

Keep Your Eye on the Goal

No one can cause you to have any kind of emotional reaction without your first giving them permission to do so. You alone are responsible for your feelings and emotions. When you know what you plan to do with your life, you will not allow annoying situations to deter you from your goals for long. If you set ambitious goals for yourself and work enthusiastically toward them, you will quickly realize that you don't have time to allow petty annoyances to upset you and keep you from your objectives.

Today's action for success:

Never let others distance you from your goal. People can be petty, and at times wish another ill will. This can occur by attempts to distract a person from his mission in life. If all the pettiness and distractions are allowed into a person's life, the mission never grabs hold. We become players in our own soap opera. Be supportive of others in their roles. Help them willingly with achieving a goal that may be too large for them to handle. Be there to assist. Build up others and do not tear them down.

COOPERATION

Try telling your boss about the things you like, and see how willingly he or she will help you get rid of the things you don't like.
—NAPOLEON HILL

Be Your Own Boss

In recent years, great strides have been made in overcoming the traditional adversarial relationship between workers and bosses. At last we're learning that when we focus on better serving our clients and customers, everybody wins. When you begin to focus on what's good in your company instead of what you don't like, you will be amazed how quickly you will have more responsibility, and soon you will be teaching your employees how to do your old job.

Today's action for success:

Proactive behavior is a winning move. Let your boss know what you are good at, and you will be able to cultivate those things you like to do more often. Complainers do not attract the good will of bosses because when a complainer shares his complaints all the boss can see is more work. But, when a person who indicates that he likes his job speaks up, the boss listens because he is tuned into how this can enable more good things to happen. The old song about "Accentuate the Positive, Eliminate the Negative" works wonders on the job.

COOPERATION

Unlimited power may be available when two or
more people coordinate their thoughts and
actions in a spirit of perfect harmony for
the attainment of a definite purpose.
—NAPOLEON HILL

Make Magic

Most of us are incapable of "going it alone." Whether it is in our careers, our personal relationships, or in life, we all need others if we are to achieve the level of success we desire. Besides, what's the point of having it all if we have no one we care about to share it? You may choose to work with others, you may ignore them, or you may choose to work against them, but the greatest successes in life come to those who work harmoniously with others. When your personal goals coincide with those of another, not only does the power of your combined labors benefit you, but such cooperation also creates a synergistic effect that allows you to achieve far more than the simple sum of your individual efforts. Know that friendship freely given and gratefully received is one of life's greatest gifts.

Today's action for success:

When you want to achieve something quickly and competently, call on the superpowers of a Mastermind Alliance. When properly created to assist in your goal, this group can work wonders for you and for themselves. They have a vested interest in seeing you succeed. This is the proverbial win-win situation that leaves no losers in the dust. A Mastermind Alliance is not a team! It is far beyond a team in its scope. It delivers where teams fail.

Create one, join one, experience one, and you will forever understand the difference. But first, determine the mission for your Mastermind Alliance because without a mission there is no purpose for this group. Make the mission a big one!

COOPERATION

Those who can't take directions graciously
have no business giving them.
—NAPOLEON HILL

Pleasing Personality

If you are an irresponsible or argumentative worker who cannot accept instructions from others, you are destined to remain at the bottom of the workforce. Before you can ever hope to manage other people, you must learn to manage yourself and your relationships with others effectively, particularly with those in higher positions in the organization. Unless you can learn how to manage your relationship with your own boss or bosses, you will never be able to manage a relationship with your subordinates.

Today's action for success:

Charles Schwab worked for Andrew Carnegie. Some years he was given a million dollar bonus because he used his personality to sway the workers that Carnegie relied upon. Charles Schwab cultivated himself before he attempted to wield his power over others. He determined to become the very best, and in doing so people listened to him. Carnegie recognized his expertise and rewarded him abundantly. A pleasing personality can do far more good for you than all the knowledge in the world. If you can't interact with people, you are relatively useless to an employer. Cultivate the traits of a pleasing personality and smile yourself into a better position.

Encouragement

"We will soon be having lots of money. Leave it to me to get it, but meanwhile encourage me and tell me you think I can do it. You have no idea what it is like when not a soul on earth encourages you, and all the negative forces pour in on you. It takes super-human strength of will to throw them off. I would give anything if I had someone, even though they did not mean it or believe it, to tell me that they KNEW I COULD SUCCEED. I would like to hear this every day, and sometimes twice a day. I keep telling myself this, but it is not as if it came from an outsider. That other self in me keeps denying it when I say it. I suppose you understand what I am talking about, or DO YOU? If you do then you can sympathize with me, and perhaps you will help me. All I need is a little encouragement right now, and I will go over in a big way and bring home the bacon."

Letter written by Napoleon Hill on February 18, 1925 to Mrs. Florence Hill from Cleveland, Ohio.

ENCOURAGEMENT

Making life "easy" for children usually
makes life "hard" for them in adulthood.
–NAPOLEON HILL

Gifts for a Lifetime

Del Smith, the millionaire founder and chairman of Evergreen International Aviation, has often said, "Thank God I was born poor; I learned how to work." Like many others who made it to the top on their own, Smith believes that the greatest gift that can be given to a child is to teach him or her the value of work. It is a gift that can never be lost or stolen. It's a natural desire of parents to give their children material things they didn't have as children. Such generosity, however, often deprives children of the greatest gift you can give them: confidence in their ability to take care of themselves. When you make life "hard" for your children by requiring them to learn the value of work, they will have a far greater likelihood of success as adults.

Today's action for success:

Things that you earn for yourself are regarded far more highly than those things that are handed to you on a silver platter. Pride can be taken in personal accomplishments that consistently move us forward to our long term goals. These accomplishments indicate that the "can do" part of our personality is operational and performing well. This personal initiative is fueled by self-encouragement as well as encouragement from others. What we think we can do, we easily accomplish. There are times, however, when the well of our own encouragement runs dry and we rely on the encouragement others freely give to us. To be beneficial this encouragement must be sincere. Superficial encouragement is shallow and does nothing to propel us forward. Encouragement, to be meaningful, must be sincere and from the heart. It is a priceless gift that fortifies us for the long haul ahead. The word "courage" is taken from the French word meaning heart. When you encourage someone you literally give them a stronger heart which assists them in accomplishing their objective. Who can you "en-hearten" today? Why not begin with someone close by, notice their immediate need, and give them a gift of heart that will strengthen them in time of trouble?

ENCOURAGEMENT

Most of us don't mind being told of our faults if the critic is generous enough to mix in a few of our virtues as well.
—NAPOLEON HILL

Praise Virtues

It's a normal reaction to defend ourselves and our behavior when someone criticizes us—even if we secretly recognize that what we're being told is correct. Those who achieve great success in life, however, are those who have learned to set aside their emotions and learn from others, even when the message is unpleasant. If you find yourself being evaluated by someone else, tell yourself that criticism of some aspect of your performance is not a personal attack. Control your emotional reaction and adopt useful ideas even though you may dislike the manner in which the information is delivered.

Today's action for success:

Praise rather than criticize. Criticism never works. When you are a faultfinder rather than a "good-finder," the receiver of your criticism not only resents the message, but can come to resent you as well. That compounds the problem and is not the end you may wish to achieve. By focusing on the good aspects of an individual, with praise and encouragement, you are able to grow those elements and diminish the not-so-good ones. For example, if you know someone who is not organized but very creative, encourage the creativity and downplay the lack of organization. The realization will come that in order to be successful in the area of creativity, organization will have to come into play since long term success cannot be achieved without both.

ENCOURAGEMENT

The worst thing about worry is that it attracts
a whole flock of relatives.
—NAPOLEON HILL

Why Worry?

Worries, like sheep, seem to flock together. One worry leads to another, and soon you are overwhelmed with the potential for problems. When you allow yourself to play the "what if?" game—to speculate about additional problems that one potential problem might cause—worries multiply, each making the next seem worse.

If you must play the "what if?" game, play it to win. Focus on solutions, not on the problems themselves and the additional problems they might create. However serious your worries may seem when they awaken you at midnight, if you analyze them carefully, you will find that every problem has a solution.

Today's action for success:

Have you ever exchanged your problems with someone else? It can be both productive and enlightening. During class, we form small groups and write down a problem that we have been unable to solve. Next, problems are exchanged with group members and several solutions are written down from the reviewer's perspective. Finally, the problems together with the potential solutions are given back to the original owner. When considered this way, the emotional attachment is removed from the problem and solutions can really be found if the problem owner wants to accept them. What unsolvable problems do you have? Maybe your problem has become a friend. Encourage yourself to let go of your problem and the worry that accompanies it. You will then free up your life for more constructive work.

ENCOURAGEMENT

If you can't manage your own mental attitude,
what makes you think you can manage others?
—NAPOLEON HILL

Role Model or Bad Example

Why is it that often those who believe they would be the best managers of others—if they were only given the opportunity—haven't learned to manage themselves properly? Before you can ever have any hope of managing others effectively, you must first learn to set an example for others to follow. It is simply impossible for you to inspire others to high levels of achievement if you cannot inspire yourself to do the same. Don't make the mistake that many others make by saying, "When they make me a manager, I'll show them I can manage." The first move is yours. You must first prove yourself worthy.

Today's action for success:

You are being watched. Keep that in mind as you perform your job. Also, if you want something done, refrain from telling someone what it is you want—show them instead. A good leader becomes a good leader by first being a good follower. Learn the job and its duties, and then as you ascend the ladder of success make certain that those on the rung beneath you have solid footsteps to follow. Hardly anyone will refuse to do a job if they are capable, have a good model to follow, and are directed in a friendly, positive manner. That's success from the top down.

ENCOURAGEMENT

A positive mind finds a way it can be done.
A negative mind looks for all the ways it can't be done.
—NAPOLEON HILL

Plus or Minus?

Someone once said, "There are no truths; there are only perceptions of truth." Whether or not you accept this statement, whatever you believe to be true will become your reality. Your subconscious mind will believe anything you tell it—if you repeat the words often and with conviction. When you are faced with a daunting task that you've never attempted before, focus on the potential for success, not on the possibilities for failure. Break the job down into smaller elements and tackle each one separately. The only difference between success and failure in any job is your attitude toward it.

Today's action for success:

An "I can do it" attitude always leads to success. Being aware that a big job is just a series of smaller ones broken down into sequential steps makes the task less overwhelming. When interviewing an accomplished man handicapped due to polio, he remarked to me that "I can do everything anyone else can do, but it just takes me a little longer." Reflecting upon this, I saw a parallel with not only handicapped individuals, but people as they age, people as they are overworked, and others who cannot devote 100% of their time to a task until it is finished. Take a little longer and don't apologize for it. Succeed in your own time frame, not someone else's. Just make progress—don't worry about perfection. Knowing that you give yourself permission to operate in your timeframe will foster a positive mental attitude.

ENCOURAGEMENT

Your mental attitude is the most
dependable key to your personality.
—NAPOLEON HILL

Pleasing Personality

Your view of yourself will greatly influence how others perceive you. If you are a confident, cheerful, positive person, your co-workers, friends, and family will be attracted to your personality. If you are unhappy, negative, and always complaining about your situation, others will be repelled. Even when at times you don't feel very happy, by forcing yourself to behave in a positive fashion, you will find that you soon feel genuinely upbeat, because your subconscious mind doesn't know the difference between an artificial emotion and the real thing. When you behave positively, you will positively influence everyone around you—including yourself.

Today's action for success:

Smile and your subconscious mind believes you to be happy and you become so! This is not a trick of mental gymnastics, but a proven reality. Our subconscious mind does not know right from wrong, real from artificial, or imagination from reality. Emerson states, "Do the thing and you will have the power." This is so because the very act of doing sends a message to our subconscious mind that we are serious about this activity, and in response the subconscious mind accepts its orders. What you think about you become. Thinking makes it so. Thoughts are things. All of these statements when undertaken and understood program our mental computers to do whatever it is we command. So, to have an attractive personality, act as if you do and your subconscious will make it so.

ENCOURAGEMENT

Remember that no one is ever rewarded or promoted because of a bad disposition and a negative mental attitude.
—NAPOLEON HILL

Accentuate the Positive

If you really examine any well-managed organization, you will find that the people who are most successful are those who are positive and helpful, people who always find the time to offer encouragement and praise when it is deserved. The people who occupy the top positions are almost always happy, enthusiastic people who encourage others to behave in the same way. Yet there are always a few individuals who never seem to get the message and behave as though they can complain their way to the top.

There isn't a single situation in your career, your relationships with others, or in your personal life that benefits from a negative attitude. All will be greatly improved if you make it a practice to approach life in a positive way.

Today's action for success:

Our mind can only act on one thought at a time, so it might as well be a positive one. Just try holding two opposing ideas equally for any given time in your mind and you will see that it is difficult and will never produce action. Because, when action is taken, it will either be on one thought or the other—not both. Therefore, in order to produce positive results we should choose the positive action. This seems elementary, but if you want to be on the winning side, the only action that is sure to succeed is a positive one.

ENCOURAGEMENT

Don't look to the stars for the cause of your
misfortunes look to yourself to get better results.
–NAPOLEON HILL

Be Your Own Fortuneteller

There are many things you cannot control, but you can control the only things that really matter: your mind and your attitude. External forces have very little to do with success. Those who program themselves for success find a way to succeed even in the most difficult of circumstances. Solutions to most problems come from one source and one source alone: yourself.

Living life to the fullest is a lot like shooting the rapids in a rubber raft. Once you've made the commitment, it's difficult to change your mind, turn around, and paddle upstream to placid waters. But it's the excitement and adventure that make it all worthwhile. If you never make the attempt, you may never know the depths of despair, but neither will you experience the exhilaration of success.

Today's action for success:

Forecast your own destiny by being active in your life. Living a life fully requires participation on your part. Just being an observer, an armchair traveler, or an individual who never decides to decide, will leave you standing on the sidelines. Get involved. Make a decision—even if it's the wrong one. To be a winner you must run the race. Have you signed up?

ENCOURAGEMENT

Self-respect is the best means of getting the respect of others.
—NAPOLEON HILL

R-E-S-P-E-C-T

Have you known people who can't stand to be alone for any length of time? The chances are good that those folks don't like themselves very much. They need others around constantly to validate their own existence. Sadly, the people who need others the most are usually those whom others least like to be around. Because they don't like themselves, other people seldom do either. The surest way to command the respect of others is to become a person you like being around. Identify the characteristics you admire in others and make a conscious effort to develop them yourself. Your self-respect begins to grow the moment you decide to take the first step toward becoming the kind of person you know you can be.

Today's action for success:

Cultivate your own friendship first. You are the person that you have to be with for the rest of your life. Be certain that you like yourself. Next, treat yourself well because by doing so you can then be freed up to be kind to others. We cannot give what we lack. In order to give, we must have a supply of whatever it is we are giving out. Self-esteem and respect are inside jobs. Respect yourself by liking who you are. Take time to care about the inner you and the outer you will shine brightly because of the little candle you keep lit within.

ENCOURAGEMENT

It takes more than a loud voice to gain respect for authority.
—NAPOLEON HILL

Be a Care-Giver!

Margaret Thatcher once observed that being powerful is like being a lady: If you have to tell others you are, you aren't. Truly great leaders gain respect by the way they conduct themselves, not by the loudness of their orders. You gain respect by respecting others. Follow the Golden Rule in your treatment of others, and you will win their undying loyalty.

If you ever expect to have authority over others, you must first prove yourself worthy. You must demonstrate to them that you care about them, that as their leader you will always look out for their interest. A good officer always makes sure the troops are provided for before be takes care of his own needs. It's a lesson that all too often is lost in the scramble to get to the top—but one that will most certainly undercut your progress if you overlook it.

Today's action for success:

It's a fact that the more people you care about the more people care about you. When you identify another's need and work to fill it, you become a co-creator of their life. By doing the little things with care and concern for another person, you not only encourage them but give them the tools they need as well. Caring about others creates a circle of involvement that is undying.

ENCOURAGEMENT

It is always safe to talk about others as long as you speak of their good qualities.
—NAPOLEON HILL

Be a Good-Sayer

The old adage "If you can't say something nice about someone, don't say anything at all" is especially valid today. In any organization, regardless of size, the rumor mill works overtime when it comes to negative gossip. And you can be sure that unkind things you say about others will very quickly find their way to them, for it is also a truism that those who talk about others to us, talk about us to others. Not only should you not speak badly of others—you should not participate in conversations in which others do. Spend your time with those who focus on important things, and you will never have to apologize for an unkind word uttered in a moment of weakness.

Today's action for success:

Do you ever notice how certain people remain quiet when others are being openly discussed? They appear to have nothing to say or to contribute. This could be because they are refraining from making a negative statement and prefer to opt out of the conversation. Two negatives do not equal a positive when gossiping about people. Those who focus on the positive know this and do not engage their energies in such negative talk. Stay quiet, walk away, or just change the subject, but do not participate in general gossip or you may find yourself being the next topic of discussion.

ENCOURAGEMENT

Instead of complaining about what you don't like about your job, start commending what you do like and see how quickly it improves.
–NAPOLEON HILL

Why I Like My Job

It's easy to find fault with any job. Whatever your occupation or profession, there are always some unpleasant and mundane tasks you would rather omit. It is also easy to allow the things you dislike to dominate your thoughts and for you to overlook the fact that the things you dislike about your work are really a very small percentage of the overall job. Make it a point to find something good in your job every day. It need not be a big, important event; simply finding joy in doing one thing particularly well will suffice. Then, instead of looking forward to the end of the day, you will find yourself actually looking forward to going to work.

Today's action for success:

The old saying states: We don't know what we have until it's gone. That is very true in all areas of employment. Many people declare to the Universe that their job is the worst one on the planet, but allow them to lose it and they forlornly look at the door closed behind them. Why not start now and make a list of all the good things that your job offers you? I know that just off the top of your head you can come up with 5-10 reasons that your job is a keeper! If not, a lack of reasons might give you the incentive to look for a job that is more supportive.

ENCOURAGEMENT

You can do it if you believe you can.
—NAPOLEON HILL

Conceive, Believe, Achieve

It's called a "self-fulfilling prophecy" when something occurs because we believe it will. The mind is constructed so that it constantly seeks to bring into physical reality the things it thinks about most. Most of us will never realize the tremendous potential we possess—because we are unwilling to believe that we can accomplish things that others believe are impossible. "Impossible" jobs require more effort and greater concentration, but when they are completed, the rewards—both financial and psychic—are commensurate with the effort required. You may not be able to achieve everything you'd like, but you won't accomplish anything unless you believe you can.

Today's action for success:

What does it take to achieve a goal? It takes an idea, a belief, and an action. Many people stop short of the action ingredient and hope that belief will see them through to the outcome. In fact, Napoleon Hill said that 98% of the population behaved this way when dealing with their definite major purpose. It would be like leaving the ham out of the ham and eggs, the turkey out of the turkey and dressing, or the chicken out of the chicken and dumplings. With one major ingredient missing, the product is not the same. If you want to follow your recipe for success exactly, you must know the ingredients and then assemble them according to the directions. Nothing less will work.

ENCOURAGEMENT

You come finally to believe anything you tell yourself often enough—even if it is not true.
—NAPOLEON HILL

Truth or Consequences

If you repeat something over and over to yourself, your subconscious mind will eventually begin to accept it as fact. When something has been accepted as truth by your subconscious mind, it will work overtime to transform the idea into physical reality. You can take advantage of this by programming your mind to think positive thoughts. Use self-motivators or affirmations to persuade your subconscious that you are capable of doing anything you wish. Repeat the self-motivator several times a day until it becomes an automatic reaction to recall a positive phrase whenever you begin to doubt yourself. Replace "I can't" with "I will!"

Today's action for success:

Use your subconscious mind as your call to arms. Program yourself for success in the area of your choice. To instill a "can't fail" attitude into your thoughts, continually use automatic reminders that you will succeed. By repeating little thoughts like "I think I can, I think I can" and "Do it now," we strengthen our mental programs for success. Empower yourself through repetition of positive phrases that condition you to advance. Think you can and you will make it so. Remember, "What the mind can conceive and believe, the mind can achieve."

ENCOURAGEMENT

Might throws itself on the side of those who believe in right.
—NAPOLEON HILL

What Goes Around Comes Around

We human beings are the only creatures on earth who have the capacity for belief. That capacity, combined with our almost innate capability to distinguish right from wrong, provides us with a formidable power in our quest for a richer, more rewarding life. When you set goals for yourself, make sure they are based on doing the right thing for your family, your friends, your employees, and yourself. When others see that you are fair and just in your dealings with them and that you are a generous, principled person, they will move heaven and earth for you.

Today's action for success:

Create a reciprocal action that supports another as well as yourself. Do something for someone, and they in turn will do something for you. This is the Law of Karma in operation. What you put out you get back. Give good, good returns to you. Give bad, and bad manifests in your life. When this Law is understood, life changes because we realize that we can change life for our betterment. It is easy to find fault, point it out, and expect the recipient to reward us as if it were lost. Unfortunately, there are no rewards for fault finding. People resent hearing someone else's opinion of their poor behavior and turn the tables by finding fault with them. This creates a downward spiral. Create upward mobility by focusing on the positive and growing it to a bountiful harvest.

Faith

Close the door of fear behind you and see
how quickly the door to faith will open in front of you.
—NAPOLEON HILL

You never can tell when you do an act
Just what the result will be;

But with every deed you are sowing a seed
Though the harvest you may not see.

Each kindly act is an acorn dropped
In God's productive soil;

You may not know, but the tree shall grow
With shelter for those who toil.

You never can tell what your thought will do
In bringing you hate or love,

For thoughts are things and their airy wings
Are swifter than carrier doves.

They follow the law of the universe—
Each thing must create its kind,

And they speed o'er the track to bring you back
Whatever went out from your mind.

—ELLA WHEELER WILCOX

Source: *PMA Science of Success*. 1983. Pgs. 117 & 118.

FAITH

A most beneficial use of time is silent meditation,
while searching for guidance from within.
—NAPOLEON HILL

Meditate

We all experience rare moments when a blinding revelation comes to us, when we suddenly see things differently than ever before. Usually, however, we learn the truth about ourselves gradually, over long periods of time, from quiet introspection. We are all spiritual, but some of us have learned to tap more effectively into the great strength that resides in the spiritual portion of ourselves.

The spirit is not boisterous and noisy. Getting in touch with your spiritual self demands tranquility and solitude. Make sure you dedicate a portion of every day to thought and study, to think and reflect upon your life. Choose a time and place that best allow you to relax your mind and devote your thoughts to reflection.

Today's action for success:

The practice of meditation is diverse. Select a method and place that suits your personality and just begin. Set aside thirty minutes a day for quiet reflection. You may simply think about a quotation, an experience from your day, or something that you are grateful for in your life. Think about what this aspect of your life contributes to your well-being. Meditation can happen while walking, sitting, or quietly reclining. However you decide to pursue going to that quiet, internal spot, practice this journeying each day. It will clear your mind and renew your spirit. Afterwards, ask yourself what you have learned from the practice. Perhaps jot down a few sentences in a special journal that summarizes your meditation. And, then begin again tomorrow.

FAITH

The greatest cure known for loneliness,
discouragement, and discontentment
is work that produces a healthy sweat.
—NAPOLEON HILL

Labor to the Rescue

Emotions are sometimes strange, volatile, and unpredictable. They do not always respond to logic and reason. They do, however, respond to action. If you have occasional feelings of loneliness, discouragement, or discontentment, the best way to kill such negative emotions is to work them to death. Almost nothing is as bad as it first seems, and there's nothing like a hard day's work to put everything in proper perspective.

When you begin to feel negative emotions, dwelling on your misfortunes only makes you feel worse. Do your best to put them out of your mind and think about more positive, constructive things. Physical labor can help. Choose a task that doesn't require a great deal of concentration, and then focus on accomplishing the task at hand.

Today's action for success:

First invite Faith into your day. As Dr. Hill states, "Faith is fear in reverse." If we are fearful we are not being faithful. Depression is an expression of fear that has grown into an emotion. In order to dissolve this negative feeling, the advice that works is a form of action known by some as mindless labor. Get busy doing something that requires little thinking but is strong on action. Wash the floor on your hands and knees, clean the windows until they sparkle, mow the grass and delight in the earthy smell, and even wash and dry dishes.

Work can always be a labor of love. By acting we send a message to our brain that we will not succumb to the paralyzing emotion of depression. Give yourself the power to choose your own best attitude.

FAITH

A negative mind spawns only negative ideas.
—NAPOLEON HILL

Use Your Inner Voice

It is a physical impossibility for a negative mind to generate positive thoughts. When you allow yourself to dwell on the negative aspects of life, negative thinking expands to fill all of your thoughts until there is no room for positive thoughts to grow. It becomes an endless cycle. The habit of negative thinking generates more and more negative thoughts, which the mind attempts to turn into physical reality. The result is a life of despair and hopelessness. Develop the habit of eliminating negative thoughts the moment they appear. Start small at first. When you first hear that inner voice that says, "I can't do this," put the thought out of your mind immediately. Instead, concentrate on the task itself. Break it down into manageable parts and complete them one at a time. When the job is finished, tell your doubting self: "You were wrong. I could do it, and I did!"

Today's action for success:

Don't let your inner critic direct the movie of your life. You—and only you—produce the results you want. When your critic says, "You can't do this," respond by saying in a self-assured loud voice "Watch me!" Giving your critic his walking papers frees you to become all that you want to be. Have faith in your ability to accomplish whatever dream moves you to action.

FAITH

It doesn't pay to look at others through a foggy mental attitude.
—NAPOLEON HILL

Keep the Fog at Bay

You must keep your mind sharply focused on your goals, and you must have a grounding philosophy that sustains you when the going is tough. When you apply the principles of success consistently until they become a part of you, no longer will you have to stop and think about what you should do in any given situation. Your positive response will be automatic.

Make sure you spend time in reflection and study. Clearly establish your goals and develop a plan and timetable for their achievement. Read the works of motivational writers and the great philosophers, and use the knowledge you gain to develop your own code of conduct. Establish your own philosophy of success that you can stick with—day in and day out—regardless of what the rest of the world does.

Today's action for success:

Have faith that you can clearly see your ultimate purpose in life and that you can place yourself firmly on the path to your destination. Project yourself into your future clearly and positively and envision where you want to be at a given point in time. Use all your senses to call this image into being. Now, when you have it placed clearly in your mind's eye, begin to walk toward it in reality. Soon you will be ascending the steps to the new you.

FAITH

A positive mental attitude is an irresistible force
that knows no such thing as an immovable body.
—NAPOLEON HILL

Focus to Move Mountains

Time and again we hear stories about ordinary people who do seemingly impossible things when they find themselves in an emergency situation. They perform Herculean feats of strength and endurance, things they never dreamed they were capable of doing. Wouldn't it be wonderful if you could harness that strength and make it available anytime you need it? You can—if you believe you can.

No doubt you can remember a time in your life when you were exceptionally focused on your objective, a time when you achieved more in less time than ever before. Perhaps it was an impending vacation that motivated you to get everything done before you departed, or perhaps it was a "must pass" exam that helped you focus your concentration. The intensity that you developed in those situations is always available to you when you have a Positive Mental Attitude.

Today's action for success:

Faith allows us to focus on a given outcome with intensity. By having faith and holding this belief strongly in our hearts, we are able to summon energy that was not centered in us before. The act of believing locks us in to universal forces such as the law of attraction and permits us to gather momentum toward our desired outcome. This momentum is energy. As the energy accumulates, it fuels our burning desire. The more fuel or emotion we can stockpile for our task, the quicker we will achieve. The catalyst is faith. And, faith followed by action makes us a sure winner every time.

FAITH

If you are sure you are right,
you need not worry what the world thinks.
—NAPOLEON HILL

If Confident Move Forward

If you are ever to achieve noteworthy success in your life, you must be willing to stand apart from the crowd. Success is something that is achieved by the minority, not the majority, of people. You will also discover as you climb the ladder of success that there are many who, out of jealousy or envy, will belittle your achievements. Nevertheless, if you have the courage of your convictions, nothing can deter you from your course. You develop confidence in your beliefs by doing your own thinking and by constantly testing and revising your knowledge. Use W. Clement Stone's R2A2 Principle to Recognize and Relate, Assimilate and Apply information from any field to help solve your problems and direct your thinking.

Today's action for success:

The most important person that you can have faith in is YOU! If you doubt your worth or your ability to accomplish whatever you put your mind to, you will not achieve it. Self-doubt is defeating because you affirm to your subconscious mind your desire to fail. In order to succeed, you must remove all traces of self-doubt. Tell yourself, repeatedly, that you can and do succeed at will. Replace thoughts of self-doubt with thoughts of success due to your can-do attitude.

FAITH

Most illness begins with a negative mind.
—NAPOLEON HILL

Cure Your Mind First

It's been proven again and again. Hypochondriacs, people who are convinced that they are sick even though nothing is wrong with them, experience the exact symptoms of the actual illness. For them, the illness is just as real as if their bodies were ravaged by disease. It is also possible to make yourself ill through constant worry and fear of failure, because the mind constantly strives to turn into reality the things we think about most. Protect your mental health with the same care you give your physical body. Just as your body requires healthy, nourishing foods, and a balanced diet, so does your mind. Make sure you feed it plenty of positive thoughts.

Today's action for success:

Medicine today is finally acknowledging the mind connection to health. Continual thoughts of illness, disease, and general feelings of illness always complicate and impede the healing process. Emil Coué's affirmation, "Every day in every way I get better and better" is the daily dose of your mental vitamin that you should take immediately upon awakening. Prescribe it for yourself and assess the difference after one month. As you brush your teeth each morning, use this affirmation to brush ill health out of your mind. It's the best tonic you can take. Truly it can be the elixir of life.

FAITH

Individuals with positive mental attitudes are never found in a rut.
—NAPOLEON HILL

Stay Out of the Rut

Individuals with a positive attitude are those who somehow always manage to find something new and interesting even in the most mundane tasks. They don't allow themselves to be bored, because they are always seeking ways to do things faster, better, and more efficiently. If you make it a practice to find better ways to do the same old things, you will soon be marked for advancement. You will be supervising others who are performing your old job because you've proven that you are a person who can be counted on to take the initiative and do what needs to be done without being told.

Today's action for success:

Faith in things unseen gets us out of ruts quickly because by envisioning the unseen, we then create the seen. Creative imagination relies on faith to plant the seed of an idea in a person's mind. When that seed is nurtured, cultivated, and grown, the end result is a new way of doing something that originated because of your applied faith. In order to get out of a rut, envision yourself free of the limitation and then question yourself as to how you got to be at the top of the hill rather than at the bottom of the rut. Think backwards, live forwards.

FAITH

If you don't believe it yourself, don't ask anyone else to do so.
—NAPOLEON HILL

Believe and Achieve

It is virtually impossible not to transmit your doubts and insecurities to others through body language, tone of voice, inflection, word choice, and other subtle characteristics. When you show by your actions that you lack self-confidence, other people also begin to doubt your ability to perform. You can gain the respect and confidence of others. Begin by making a list of all the things you like about yourself and the things you would like to change. Make a conscious effort to build upon your positive strengths and correct your weaknesses. It may not be easy, but if you assess yourself objectively and persevere in your efforts, you will eventually prevail.

Today's action for success:

Sometimes others can be the keeper of our beliefs for us when our light wanes, but not for long. Friends and families can serve as memory reminders when we temporarily forget about our greatness. This is a way of bolstering one another up when an individual is going through a loss or crisis. When we listen to success stories about ourselves that others recite, their memory activates our mind to recall these events. When reminded of our life's story, we will hopefully be compelled to continue on with renewed enthusiasm. In order to keep your candle lit, you must guard the flame. Another can be on watch temporarily if you take a break, but the duty ultimately is your own.

FAITH

If you don't know why you failed,
you are no wiser than when you began.
—NAPOLEON HILL

Is Repetition the Key?

There's an old adage that those who refuse to learn from history are doomed to repeat it. So it is with our failures. Unless we learn from our mistakes, we are likely to repeat them until we learn from such experiences and correct our course—or give up and accept temporary defeat as permanent failure. Every setback you encounter in life contains valuable information that, if you study it carefully, will eventually lead you to success.

Without adversity, you would never develop wisdom, and without wisdom, success would be short lived indeed. When you make a mistake, say, "That's good! I've gotten that out of the way. I will never do that again." You will no doubt make other mistakes, but they won't bother you nearly as much when you treat them as learning experiences.

Today's action for success:

Allow no one to set up limitations for you. When you share your definite major purpose too freely, others feel inclined to criticize your best efforts and tell you that you are not capable. When someone states that you are not qualified, ask them how they know. This simple question will cause them to reflect and sputter out an answer. Listen carefully, and you will find that almost always their declaration is based on opinion rather than fact. Opinions are worthless since they are a cheap commodity. Smile, and continue on with your mission knowledgeable in the fact that you will persist and succeed.

FAITH

Never tear down anything unless you are
prepared to build something better in its place.
—NAPOLEON HILL

Build rather than Destroy

This rule applies to both individuals and things. It's easy to criticize other people thoughtlessly for their shortcomings, and equally easy to find fault in their work or in situations that are not to your liking. It is far more difficult to be a builder of people and to create works of art, useful products, or profitable businesses. Make sure you are a builder, not a destroyer of people and things.

When you criticize the actions or work of others—your children, your employees, or others for whom you are responsible—make sure your criticisms are positive and directed at the act, or the opportunity for improvement, not the individual. Include specific suggestions for their application and focus on the potential for success.

Today's action for success:

Never criticize. It does not work. People resent hearing what they already know. Rather, praise the qualities you like in an individual and you will see more of this characteristic. Catch people doing something good, acknowledge that aspect, and build on the traits that you want to reinforce. Criticism focuses on the negative, while praise focuses on the positive. Use positive reinforcement whenever you are able.

FAITH

Be sure about what you want from life and
doubly sure of what you have to give in return.
–NAPOLEON HILL

First Give, Second Get

Examine the lives of successful people, and you will find that they have paid a price that is in direct proportion to the amount of success they have earned. Close examination will almost always reveal years of study and preparation before great success is achieved. This principle is consistent in virtually every field of individual achievement—in the arts, medicine, science, or business. Nothing worthwhile ever comes easily.

As you consider your own goals, also consider what you are willing to sacrifice for what you expect to receive. You should be prepared to give generously of your time and talents long before expecting a return on your investment. Many "overnight successes" labored in obscurity for many years before they were finally recognized for their achievements.

Today's action for success:

It is in giving that we receive, or so the Bible says. Dr. Hill states that we must give in advance of achieving in proportion to our definite major purpose. In essence, Dr. Hill believes that we must put out service in advance in order to be compensated with success. The amount of return we desire must be paid for in advance through work, service, or other means. Nothing comes of nothing.

FAITH

The value of actions depends on the courage they require.
—NAPOLEON HILL

Your Capacity for Greatness

Ordinary people who do extraordinary things for others are those we later call heroes. When asked why they performed as they did, they often say, "It was nothing anyone else wouldn't have done in the circumstances." Perhaps that's their way of saying we all have the capacity for greatness. It is only when we are severely tested that we rise to the occasion and perform at the highest levels of our competence.

You become a person who does the right things when presented with great opportunities the same way you achieve success at anything: through force of habit. If you make it a practice to take the appropriate action even when it seems unimportant and insignificant, you will do the right thing—without thinking—in important situations. If you let your actions speak for you, you will never have to worry about others recognizing your contribution.

Today's action for success:

Actions are like lightning. They impact our lives. Hearing the role of thunder may arouse fear, but when lightning hits with an impact people take notice. Actions are observable and measurable. People watch and record what others do. By taking action, we focus the camera of our life. Lightning strikes where you take action.

FAITH

If you think you can buy your way into heaven with money alone, you may regret that you didn't convert it into good deeds instead.
—NAPOLEON HILL

Deed to Heaven

If through some terrible, unforeseen tragedy you should die tomorrow, how would your epitaph read? What would others remember about you? In the final analysis, you will be remembered for your good works, not for the money you have accumulated during your lifetime. Your wealth may be little more than the cause for disagreements among your heirs, while your good deeds will be remembered long after you are gone. As you accumulate wealth, devote a portion of your money and your time to causes that benefit those less fortunate than you.

Today's action for success:

Look at your age today, add on the years you expect to live, and write down your projected year of death. How many years are between where you are now and your year of death? Staring you in the face is the opportunity that awaits you. Whether it's 2, 12, or 25 years remaining in your life, you can still focus on doing all the good that you can do with the time remaining. Ask yourself, how many summers do you have left and how do you want to spend them? Birthdays? Holidays? Family reunions? You get the idea. The message is that you must busy yourself now with doing what you intended to do. Intentions are not actions. Actions are the concrete bricks that build the basement for the castle of your good deeds. Get going now—this very minute—on the foundation of your future!

FAITH

Faith is a combination of thoughts and actions.
—NAPOLEON HILL

Exercise Your Faith

When you apply your faith in yourself, your faith in your fellow man, and your faith in God, the result is a positive course of action that when persistently followed will almost always lead to success. When you believe in your ideas and in your abilities, and you trust in the Infinite Intelligence of the universe, you know that your thoughts and deeds will ultimately lead to a successful conclusion. You cannot fail.

Today's action for success:

Belief makes it so! Believe and achieve. Know that you can do it, and you will. Success grows in the garden of belief. Belief allows us to contact Infinite Intelligence directly and to use the acquired energy to manifest our dreams. Without belief, nothing happens. Believe, believe, believe.

Opportunity

The greatest of all gifts is the gift of an opportunity for a man to make good on his own merits.

Similar opportunities abound for those who have definiteness of purpose, plus the personal initiative and the creative vision and faith to embrace and act upon the opportunities. Any such person, with a sound commercial idea, can always find capital and such other means as may be needed to develop the idea. The system of free enterprise is so devised that it is constantly seeking men with sound ideas which can be commercialized. It rewards those who have the courage and the personal initiative to go after that which they desire!

Source: PMA Science of Success. 1983. Pgs. 217-218.

OPPORTUNITY

The man who dipped a chunk of ice cream in chocolate
and called it eskimo pie made a fortune for the
five seconds of imagination it took to create the idea.
—NAPOLEON HILL

Creative versus Synthetic

We are just beginning to understand the mysterious ways in which the mind works, but successful people have long known how to use the power of creative vision to their advantage. Many "new" ideas are really nothing more than a new combination of two well-known products or ideas. Nevertheless, great fortunes have been built upon such combinations when they are supported by a clever name and marketing campaign. There is a definite process that you can use to tap into your imagination. In his book *A Technique for Producing Ideas*, James Webb Young identified five steps:

1. Gather the appropriate information.
2. Work the information over in your mind.
3. Incubate the idea in your subconscious.
4. Recognize the "Eureka!" stage when the idea is born.
5. Shape and develop the idea for practical application.

The technique works. Give it a try the next time you're searching for a creative solution to an old problem.

Today's action for success:

Dr. Hill identified two types of imagination: creative and synthetic. He defines them as follows: Creative Imagination—has its base in the subconscious section of the mind, and serves as the medium by which basically new facts or ideas are revealed through the faculty of the sixth sense. Synthetic Imagination—consists of a combination of previously recognized ideas, concepts, plans or facts arranged in a new order, or put to a new use. The second type is the most common and lends itself to everyone's creative use. Tap into your synthetic imagination right now by "creating" two new products that are simply the blending of "old" products used in new ways. Follow the five idea generating steps above proposed by James Webb Young and see what you can invent!

OPPORTUNITY

Clarence Saunders made millions by borrowing
the self-help cafeteria idea for the grocery business
and naming it Piggly Wiggly. Imagination pays!
—NAPOLEON HILL

A Synthetic Idea

The founder of the Piggly Wiggly grocery chain was a low-level employee in a corner grocery when he visited a cafeteria and got the idea that the same techniques could be applied to the grocery business. He was ridiculed by experts, but he was convinced that the idea was a good one. Saunders persevered, and his adaptation of the self-service idea to the grocery business led him to become the father of the modern supermarket.

It is often true that a great idea alone is not enough to achieve success. Implementation may require as much as or more imagination than coming up with the idea originally. Those who study such things, however, report that when you have a really good idea, even if you can't prove it, you will intuitively know that it is good. If you're convinced, stick with it. Others will eventually recognize the value of your idea.

Today's action for success:

Do some research on your favorite inventors, scientists, military strategists, authors, etc. For example, Thomas A. Edison willingly shared the fact that most of his inventions actually involved nothing new, but were merely the combination of old facts to produce new results. Investigate this thought further. Historically, who else can you identify that relied on the old to create the new? Reflect on the idea that in reality there is nothing new under the sun.

OPPORTUNITY

The imagination is the workshop of the soul, where are shaped all the plans for individual achievement.
—NAPOLEON HILL

Imagine—Make It So!

Before you can build anything worthwhile, you must first create it in your mind. Your mind is not constrained by physical limitations or boundaries. In the workshop of your mind, you can visualize things that have never been. It is said that Albert Einstein visualized how the universe might look if he were riding astride a beam of light through infinity. Then he worked out the mathematics to support his theory of relativity. You can use the power of your imagination to visualize solutions to difficult problems, to develop new ideas, and to see yourself achieving the goals you have set for yourself.

Today's action for success:

Spend some time today daydreaming just for the pleasure of it. See a certain aspect of your life as it is now and then consider how you would like it to be in the future. Perhaps this involves plans for a new home, a new car, redecorating, landscaping, a second home, another degree, travel, retirement, or whatever you desire. After your daydream, wake up and begin to physically plan toward the goal you have set. A good way to begin is through the construction of a dream board or collage. These are good intermediary vehicles to begin to bring your dream to reality. Simply locate a poster board, some old magazines or picture books, and cut out pictures that match your dream and glue them to the board in a pleasing manner. Let your dream unfold. Add to it daily. Look at it daily and begin to see the possibility of your dream becoming reality in the near future.

OPPORTUNITY

Your job will never be any bigger than your imagination makes it.
—NAPOLEON HILL

Be Clear and Grand

Daniel Burnham, the turn-of-the-century architect and civic planner whose plan for the 1893 Chicago World's Fair had an enormous influence on contemporary civic design, was quoted as saying, "Make no little plans." He knew that to achieve great things we must have grand ideas. If you can imagine it, you can create it. And if you can create in your imagination the job that you would like to have, it is possible to create it in the real world.

Today's action for success:

Be crystal clear about what you desire. Make plans that are specific and goal oriented. By knowing what it is you really want, you will immediately recognize it when it appears. By naming your specific desire, you draw the reality of that desire to you in a much quicker manner because you know what you want. List makers know this to be true. When you construct either a to-do list or an I-dream list, you keep the concept of your desire front and center in your mind's eye. This draws the outcome to you sooner and in a profound way. Do not only write it down, but write it down and then stay watchful so that you will recognize it when it appears.

OPPORTUNITY

If you have a better way of doing anything,
your idea may be worth a fortune.
—NAPOLEON HILL

Possibility Thinking

In any type of business, the most valuable ideas are those that make money, save money, save time, or improve the way things are done. Every improvement, however slight, is a step in the right direction. Being alert for opportunities to improve things is a function of a positive attitude. It is virtually impossible to think creatively about opportunities when your thoughts are concentrated on the downside risk instead of the upside potential. As you search for ways to improve your performance, or to find a better, faster, or more economical way to perform a task or build a product, by all means analyze and minimize the risks but focus on the possibilities.

Today's action for success:

Can/Can't. The opposites that do not attract! If you have a "can do" attitude, you are going places. If you have a "can't do" attitude, you may as well not even show up for work. These two attitudes determine your success or failure in life. Knowing that you can succeed, predispositions you for success today and in the future. Why? Because you have assured yourself that you have the capacity to do what it is you intend to accomplish. This in itself is the best predictor of success. Knowing that you can because you have done it in the past, determines your next outcome as well. Be a believer—but most of all believe in yourself because you are your greatest asset.

OPPORTUNITY

The mind grows only through use,
And it atrophies through idleness.
—NAPOLEON HILL

Read for Mental Strength

Just as the physical body becomes strong through regular exercise, so does the mind require regular use to remain strong. Make sure that your personal development plan includes plenty of mental stimulation. One of the best ways to develop your imagination and visualization skills is through reading. As you read, your mind translates the words into images that help you better understand the concepts about which you are reading. Become a voracious reader. Read newspapers, trade magazines, self-help books, and novels; all will contribute to your store of knowledge and to your ability to visualize and more effectively use your imagination.

Today's action for success:

Undoubtedly readers are leaders. Reading fosters future potential for greatness. Those who read are those who strengthen their mental capacities. Brains that have been engaged in thought processes perform far better than the ones left to atrophy through disuse. Become excellent in your field through reading. Read what interests you, but also read in the area of your profession by subscribing to trade magazines, utilizing your library card, and using the internet for professional journals that are available online. If you read daily in your area of major interest, you will soon find yourself an authority in a matter of years. It has been said that if you read thirty minutes a day in the same professional area of interest, within three years you will be known as an expert in your community, add two more years to this for a total of five, and you will be known nationally, and finally add two more years of reading in the same subject matter area, and you will be recognized internationally. Doesn't sound like much effort, but that's just another example of how reading pays off. Practice the 3–5–7 formula and see for yourself!

OPPORTUNITY

Remember the mind grows strong through use.
Struggle makes power.
–NAPOLEON HILL

Use It or Lose It

Napoleon Hill liked to tell a story about his grandfather, a wagon builder in North Carolina. When the old man cleared the land for cultivation, he always left a few oak trees in the middle of the field at the mercy of the elements, unsheltered by other trees in the forest. It was from those trees that his grandfather made the wagon's wheels. Because they were forced to struggle against the fury of nature, they grew strong enough to bear the heaviest load.

Welcome difficult challenges, for the greatest opportunities will come from challenges that force you to expand your mind as you search for creative solutions. During life's bleakest hours, take solace in the fact that you are strengthening yourself through struggle so that in the future you will be prepared to take on even greater challenges. Like the old oak tree, you grow strong only when you are forced to struggle.

Today's action for success:

Struggle creates profound opportunities to overcome obstacles that would normally hold us back. Without struggle man grows mentally and physically weak. Struggle is the instrument nature uses to allow us to grow and eventually prosper. Victories gained without struggle are hollow because they come too easily. When you struggle and eventually accomplish your goal because you persisted, the victory is all that sweeter. Invite struggle into your life, recognize it for the gift-giver it is. When you survive struggle, you will be awarded a gift that is yours alone. Only the person who struggles and survives is awarded the prize.

OPPORTUNITY

Those who will not take a chance
Seldom have one thrust upon them.
—NAPOLEON HILL

Be a Risk-Taker

Success always involves risk. You must take a chance by investing your time, money, and effort. It pays to be thoughtful and deliberate in your analyses of opportunities, but don't let timidity hold you back.

Because you have worked hard to develop those things you must risk, it is natural for you to place a high value on them. But what use are they if you do not put them to use? You will recognize opportunity only to the extent that you are willing to consider risking your time, money, and effort. Being confident gives you the courage to face risk and act when opportunity arises. No one on earth is going to force success upon you; you will find it only to the degree that you actively seek it out.

Today's action for success:

Success plays hide and seek with many people because they do not know where to look to find it. They expect it to be handed to them on a silver platter, but when it doesn't show up there they forget to look in the cupboard! Most often success arrives in a different form than we expect it. It is not shiny and polished, but hidden in dirt and crusted over with rust. In order to uncover the hidden treasure, you must pay the price by risking your time, money, and effort in excavating the success that is hidden just below the surface. Think about the game of hide and seek you played as a child. Approach success in this manner. Know that it is there, and it is your job to find it. Leave no stone unturned, and you will ultimately achieve the success you desire.

OPPORTUNITY

This is a fine world for the person who knows precisely what he or she expects from life and is busy getting it.
—NAPOLEON HILL

No Intermission from Your Mission

We are happiest when we are striving to achieve a goal. When we achieve one goal, it's a natural human tendency to set another, usually bigger, one. W. Clement Stone calls it inspirational dissatisfaction—the letdown one experiences after a goal has been achieved and before the next step toward a new one has been taken. When you begin to experience that nagging feeling, it's time to get into action! Make sure you have a long-range plan in place so that when one short-term goal has been achieved, there is a natural progression toward the next.

Today's action for success:

Always have a new goal in your back pocket to replace the one that you have just achieved. It is good to bask in the glory of a completed goal, however, it is not good to rest on your laurels. After a short respite, it is good to get back into the saddle and begin working on another goal of equal or greater importance than the last one. Always have something to anticipate, because it keeps you focused and it keeps you young. A goal a day might just do better than the proverbial apple at keeping the doctor away!

OPPORTUNITY

Opportunity has a queer way to stalking the person who can recognize it and is ready to embrace it.
—NAPOLEON HILL

Be Prepared for Opportunities

It is a curious quirk of human nature that some people can see opportunities, while others only see problems. When you train your mind to seek out opportunities, you will find that every day literally presents you with more opportunities than you can take advantage of. They will be all around you. Instead of your seeking opportunities, they will seek you out. Your biggest problem will be choosing the best ones.

The first step in making sure you are ready to recognize opportunities when they occur is to make sure you have a clear understanding of your own core competencies. Realistically assess your strengths and weaknesses as though you were reviewing the credentials of a total stranger. Identify what areas you're best in and those where you need improvement. Work on your weaknesses and build upon your strengths so that when you recognize opportunities you are prepared to capitalize upon them.

Today's action for success:

Opportunities are around us every day, and we must be prepared to act on them when they arrive. Your level of education, state of mind, health, financial resources, and capacity to recognize an opportunity all contribute to the reception an opportunity receives. Just as in gardening, you prepare the soil before you plant the seeds. If you are not ready to accept an opportunity because of your lack of preparedness, then the loss is yours. The opportunity will go to someone else. Keep your mind poised, ready, and open, and you will be amazed at how many opportunities show up!

OPPORTUNITY

Those who are quick to see their limitations generally are slow in seeing their opportunities.
—NAPOLEON HILL

Capitalize upon Capabilities

Movie producer Michael Todd once said, "Being broke is temporary; being poor is a state of mind." So it is with opportunity. Whether you see opportunities or limitations is entirely within your control. How you view the world is a reflection of your mental attitude. If you focus on your inadequacies, you will be plagued by fear, doubt, and failure, but when you focus on your strengths, you will find courage, confidence, and success.

Self-confidence can replace self-doubt only by deliberate, planned effort. When you start to doubt your capabilities, pause to review your previous accomplishments. Identify every experience that might be helpful to you in your present situation. When you apply the knowledge and wisdom you have accumulated, there are few limitations that you cannot overcome.

Today's action for success:

Know who you are and what you stand for in life. You may be a person of many talents, but not a person of every talent. Know your strengths and also your weaknesses. Identifying each is valuable to your outcome in life because you can then forecast what it is you can and can't do effectively. Being a jack of all trades has its advantages, but knowing where to find help when you need it is even more beneficial. Wisdom requires one to know where to look for help. In everyone's life there comes a time when they must seek help. Make both options work for you.

OPPORTUNITY

Don't ever admit that the world has
not given you an opportunity.
—NAPOLEON HILL

No Fair!

Opportunities are never just handed to you; they must be created. Opportunities abound for every individual in every walk of life. They may not be the opportunities that you prefer, but each opportunity of which you take advantage leads to bigger and better opportunities. Physical and mental handicaps may mean that you have to explore territories unknown to others, but they also mean you have opportunities those others will never find. Think of Stephen Hawking's brilliant research on the nature of the universe despite the fact that a crippling disease makes writing and speaking, as we know it, impossible for him.

Those who approach their jobs and careers with enthusiasm always find plenty of opportunities, while those who complain about no one ever giving them a chance are merely observers of life. When you are determined that you will not allow others to determine your future for you, when you refuse to allow temporary setbacks to defeat you, you are destined for great success. The opportunities will always be there for you. If there are adversities that you cannot overcome right now, remember to capitalize upon them at a later date by looking for the seed of an equivalent or greater benefit.

Today's action for success:

Why does one person see an opportunity and another cannot? Possibly, it relates to having a positive outlook on life. If one can find the seed of an equal or equivalent benefit in an adversity, then that same person can recognize an opportunity in an easier fashion due to his positive outlook. Staying positive has its benefits. Mental health and physical health are improved, daily stress is reduced, and opportunities appear almost on schedule. So, in order to become more open to opportunities, a person should first focus on becoming positive. As the saying goes, positive mental attitude is the right mental attitude in all circumstances. Look at it this way. A positive mental attitude is like raising your antenna for opportunities. You know that opportunities are out there, now you have the mechanism for attracting them to you too!

OPPORTUNITY

If it isn't your job to do it, perhaps it is your opportunity.
—NAPOLEON HILL

Take the Initiative

Someone once observed that the reason we often fail to recognize opportunities is because they come disguised as problems. When a customer, a colleague, or your boss has a problem, it may create a valuable opportunity for you. It isn't important to the person with the problem how your company is organized or whose responsibility it is to solve the problem; he or she only wants the situation resolved.

The next time a customer, a colleague, or your boss asks for your assistance in something that falls outside your area of responsibility, instead of referring them to someone else, offer to help. Look at the situation from the other person's point of view. How would you like the situation handled if the roles were reversed? Take the initiative to find the answer, solve the problem, or keep the project moving forward.

Today's action for success:

We all know that what goes around comes around. When someone has a problem and you offer to help rather than shrugging your shoulders, you become part of the solution. Next time, when you have a problem and need help you will already have an Ace in reserve—the person you helped. Create a circle of friends and thereby increase your odds for success.

OPPORTUNITY

Opportunity often knocks—only to find no one in.
—NAPOLEON HILL

Knock—Knock

The world is filled with unfortunate souls who didn't hear opportunity's knock at the door because they were down at the convenience store buying lottery tickets. They have never learned that, as Branch Rickey, general manager of the Brooklyn Dodgers from 1942–50, once observed, "Luck is the residue of design." You will be surprised how much your luck will improve when you make sure you are prepared to take advantage of opportunities.

How many times have you had a great idea that you failed to act upon, only to discover later that someone used the same idea to start a business, get a promotion, or find a better job? Resolve now to get into action when you have a good idea. Don't wait for something to happen—make it happen!

Today's action for success:

It might be a good time to examine your past practices and to ask yourself whether your actions have contributed to your success or to your failure. Upon examination you may find that numerous times you obstructed your path to success. Once this is recognized and acknowledged then it is easy to identify the pattern when it appears again and work to eliminate it. Before a person can change, the need for change must be acknowledged. You are the only person who can change you. Let that inspire you to take corrective action.

OPPORTUNITY

A resourceful person will always
make opportunity fit his or her needs.
–NAPOLEON HILL

Quest for Success

The ability to recognize opportunities is a critical element of success, but it is only the beginning. An idea is valuable only if it can be put into practice—by you. Highly successful people know that there are many ways to capitalize on an opportunity. They evaluate and shape it to fit their capabilities, or they put together a team composed of people with the skills necessary to take advantage of it—whatever it takes to make it work. Seldom is there any single right answer in business. Often there are any number of right answers.

Today's action for success:

Oftentimes we believe that there is only one correct way of doing things, and that the other ways are inferior methods. This is seldom true although this belief can freeze us in our action tracks. Believing that there is one right way, many people strive for success as if they were seeking the infamous Fountain of Youth. By looking for the one right answer you might walk right past many ways that would work just as well. In your quest for success be open-minded and observant. Be a doer rather than a follower. Know where you are going, but be willing to take a few detours along the way. Finally, define success on your own terms, so that when you come upon it you will recognize it for what it really is.

Service

Render more service and better service than that
for which you are paid and sooner or later you will
receive compound interest from your investment,
for it is inevitable that every seed of useful service
you now sow will multiply itself and come
back to you in overwhelming abundance.

—NAPOLEON HILL

SERVICE

The richest persons are those who give most in service to others.
—NAPOLEON HILL

Give to Get

Financial wealth is only one measure of success. The truly happy and successful individual is the man or woman who is healthy, financially secure, challenged in his or her career, and is making a difference in the lives of others. It isn't always easy to render service to others. The world is a cynical and dangerous place where others are likely to mistrust your motives. They can be convinced only by consistent, sustained, outstanding service that is enthusiastically and cheerfully offered. In time, even the most cynical individual will come to accept your willingness to go the extra mile if you are sincere in your offers of assistance and in the service you provide.

Today's action for success:

You do not have to deliver a truckload of assistance to be considered sincere. Little opportunities for service exist daily and can be rendered in a matter of minutes. For examples, you can lend a listening ear to the person who wants to talk. Carry a bag of groceries to the car for an elderly person. Ask "May I help you?" and sincerely mean it. Call someone you haven't heard from in awhile. Say, cheerily, "It's good to hear your voice." When speaking to someone, use their name. Spark conversation by discussing a topic you know to be of personal interest to the individual. Buy a cup of morning coffee for a person who could use one. Be the first to clear the table after dinner. And, don't forget to feed the cat! Above all else, smile. These actions reward you first. This is where it counts. You must be happy before you can spread the joy.

SERVICE

Only the highway of useful service leads to the city of happiness.
—NAPOLEON HILL

Cost of Happiness

Psychologists who study human behavior have concluded that we are happiest when we are striving to achieve success. It is the act of striving, not the successful completion of the task, that provides the greatest psychic rewards. When you strive to achieve success through service to others, you multiply the benefits to yourself, and you ensure that whatever road you choose in life will ultimately lead you to success and happiness.

There is no occupation or profession that will not benefit from a concerted effort to better serve others. But the greatest benefit will be to you, in the form of the self-satisfaction that comes from knowing that you made a difference, that without you others would never have received the service you provided.

Today's action for success:

Being a doer of good deeds is worthy of praise and even a medal as many of us have witnessed in *The Wizard of Oz*. Philanthropic work is always good for the receiver and good for the provider. Decide to put yourself on the provider side of the fence and see how you doubly benefit. Not only do you improve your self-esteem through giving, but you also increase your karma. You get what you expect to receive in life, so if you are giving good things and are also expecting good things to come to you because of your actions, how can you lose? Create a circle of giving that has no discernable end or beginning. Change the world one positive deed at a time.

SERVICE

When you start giving out, you'll soon begin taking in.
—NAPOLEON HILL

What Goes Around Comes Around

There's an old folk song about a thirsty traveler who comes across a pump in the desert. An attached note explains that there's a jar of water buried nearby to prime the pump. You've got to give before you get, the note says. It is up to the traveler to decide whether to drink the water from the jar or take a chance that the small amount of water invested will result in an unlimited supply of cold, clear water.

So it is with going the extra mile. You've got to give before you get. You cannot expect to receive generous rewards and then decide what to give in return. You must give freely and have faith that the rewards will eventually come. As clergyman Frank Crane once said, "You may be deceived if you trust too much, but you will live in torment if you do not trust enough."

Today's action for success:

Dr. Crane's observation is a sound one. Try trust instead of skepticism. Even if you feel you will be taken advantage of, go the extra mile because you want to, not because someone has tricked you into doing so. Do the chore not because it's on your to-do list, but because you want to. You possess the requirements to complete the task, so with mindfulness do it for the simple joy of doing something that you are capable of doing. Praise instead of complain. Whisper instead of shout. Laugh instead of cry. Rejoice instead of lament. Love instead of hate. Remember, as Goethe states: Do the thing, and you shall have the power. The power is within you if you choose to use it.

SERVICE

If you have something you don't need, give it to someone who needs it. It will come back to you in one way or another.
—NAPOLEON HILL

Create a Better Place

You know by now how important it is to offer service freely to your community without expecting anything specific in return. You know as well how important the intangible personal benefits of self-respect and inspiration that accompany such action are.

But it is also true that by rendering a public service you have an effect on the values in your community. Your actions are a quiet but steadfast signal to others of the importance of being involved, a sign that success does not require heartless devotion to a cause and a reminder to others of the personal satisfaction you gain from your labor. You will find that you inspire others to similar actions in different areas, creating a ripple effect that extends far beyond what you alone can do. The community in which you live will become a better place, and you will be happier being a part of it.

Today's action for success:

We have all heard that imitation is the greatest form of flattery. Have you noticed anyone copying your actions? Little children mimic our behavior, and older children model what we do. It's said that imprinting occurs frequently within the animal kingdom. Likewise in the human family. Actions truly do speak louder than words so be careful of what you are broadcasting. Maybe somebody is listening and maybe they are copying what you do and what you are saying right now. If you listen, you can hear the resonance of your actions all the way into tomorrow and beyond.

SERVICE

The surest way to promote yourself is to help others get ahead.
—NAPOLEON HILL

Self-Promotion

When you go out of your way to help others get ahead, it is inevitable that they will reciprocate. When you genuinely wish others well, even though you may feel a little envious that they are advancing faster than you or gaining more recognition, they will respond accordingly. Your good deeds will encourage them to do likewise. You may never know how many people have recommended you for a job, or a promotion, or helped you in some other way because you aided them when they needed it most.

Today's action for success:

Who needs your help today? An aging parent, a lonely child, a distant friend, a colleague, or even a forgotten pet? Ask what you can do for someone else rather than always turning the attention back to yourself. Observe a need and fill it. See something that needs to be done and without being asked, do it. This creates personal initiative and fuels enthusiasm. It allows the person doing the service to take it upon himself to be pro-active in the outcome of something that he could influence. Being a person of influence begins with being a person who takes action.

SERVICE

If you are a shepherd, be the best
and you may live to own the flock.
—NAPOLEON HILL

Sheep or Shepherd?

One of the most wonderful things about life is that we are all unique with different levels of intelligence, interests, aptitudes, and desires. How dreadfully dull it would be if we all wanted to be nuclear physicists—or bakers. But, regardless of the gifts we may have received at birth and whichever skills we may have since developed, we all have the capability to be the best at what we do.

Being the best is strictly a reflection of your attitude and your desire. Whether you are a salesperson, an executive, a secretary, or an assembly-line worker, you have the capacity to be as good as you choose to be. When you become outstanding at what you do, you will discover greatly increased demand for your services. When you become the best in your line of work, you may be asked so often to help other "sheep" that you will soon own your own "flock."

Today's action for success:

In order to carry the staff, you must be the shepherd! Nobody follows sheep but sheep. Get into the habit of assuming responsibility for making an outcome happen. Observe leaders and witness their involvement with things of a constructive nature. Decide here and now to hitch your wagon to a star and to pull others along with you. Think about leaders of the pack who have brought others to greatness. They have studied men and women for the purpose of bettering themselves. People of note have something inside of them that rises to the occasion and refuses to let them quit when they could have. Successful individuals first uncover the characteristics of the individual they want to become, and then they step into position and assume the role. Everything else then falls into place. Say what you want to be and then do the things that you have to do to become it. Thinking makes it so. In the serial Star Trek, Captain Picard commands: "Make it so!" Now, you can go and do likewise.

SERVICE

The climb upward will be easier if you take others along with you.
—NAPOLEON HILL

Two by Two

When you take the initiative, you become a de facto leader whose success will depend in large measure upon your ability to inspire others to work with you. They will follow your lead when they have confidence in you and when they know they will share in your success. Few of us are good enough or lucky enough to achieve great success completely on our own. We need others to help us. When we give more in return than we ever ask of our friends and associates, not only will we be able to accomplish much more in life, but it will also make the entire experience much more enjoyable.

Today's action for success:

Practice going the extra mile. Keep a confidential record of the times when you went beyond someone's expectation. Consider how this gesture not only helped the recipient but helped you equally—or maybe even more. Analyze why this is so. It seems that all the good that we do sooner or later comes back to us wonderfully multiplied like the loaves and the fishes. This can only happen if we freely give without any expectation of return. When it is a give and take relationship, the giver already has received his reward. When the gift is spontaneous and free, it is up to the Universe to decide what gift will be delivered upon your doorstep unexpectedly—but at just the right time—in your future for your greater benefit.

SERVICE

The greatest of all success rules is this:
Do unto others as you would if you were the others.
—NAPOLEON HILL

Compassionate Commandment

The Golden Rule is more than a principle of ethical behavior; it is a dynamic force that can work good in the lives of untold numbers of people. When you make it a practice to treat others as though you were the others, you spread goodwill among people who, in turn, may be moved to do the same. By their actions, they influence still more people, who generate goodwill among even more people. This force for goodwill increases exponentially and will return to you from totally new sources. The benefit you receive from a good deed performed today by a total stranger may have been a chain reaction from long ago when you observed the Golden Rule in your own dealings with another.

Today's action for success:

We know what the ten biblical commandments for daily living are. Why not have 17 commandments for personal success? And who better to author them than you? Let's give these commandments a positive spin too by beginning with the words "Thou shall" instead of "Thou shall not." Sit down right now with pen in hand and author the words following Napoleon Hill's 17 success principles. These will serve as a guideline for your personal and professional success. Just to get you started, let's start with: Thou shall have a definite major purpose and act on it each and every day of your adult life without fail. You get the idea. Now, go for it.

SERVICE

The quality and quantity of the service you render,
plus the attitude with which you render it, determine
the amount of pay you get and the sort of job you hold.
—NAPOLEON HILL

Your Compensation

The people who are promoted to the best positions in the company are those who make it a practice to go the extra mile, to do more than they are paid to do, and to do it willingly and cheerfully. You take the first important step toward determining your own future when you make the conscious decision to approach every task with a positive outlook and to stick with the job until it is done.

If you find this attitude difficult at first, you'll discover it eventually becomes part of you. And after you begin to realize the benefits that accrue to you because you are known as someone who always gives a little extra, you wouldn't consider doing things any other way.

Today's action for success:

Ever hear the stories about people who stopped just a fraction of an inch before making it big? It's surely difficult to decide when you should cease doing something for which you are not being compensated, however, it is in your best interest to adjust your sails if things are not progressing in your favor. When you feel unrecognized, beaten down, tired to the bone, confused, fidgety, unfocused, resentful, argumentative, and joyless while involved in the project you are considering abandoning, just dump it! The release that you will feel from deciding that this is "not me" is tremendous and uplifting. Not only do you free something for someone else to take up, but more importantly you regain your peace of mind. Peace of mind is something no fortune can buy. Sometimes giving something up can bring greater compensation than holding on to it with a clenched fist.

SERVICE

Dependability is the first foundation stone of good character.
—NAPOLEON HILL

Sound Character

People of character do what they say they will do, when they say they will do it, and according to agreed-upon conditions. They are the leaders, the individuals to whom others turn for guidance because they have demonstrated that they care, that they can be trusted. If you respect yourself enough to keep commitments even when it's inconvenient to do so, others will come to respect you too.

Dependability, like any other character trait, is a habit. Begin today—at the beginning of a new you—to develop the dependability habit. If you procrastinate or find it difficult to meet your commitments, start small. Promise yourself that you will be on time, for example, and manage your time so that you are. Soon you will find that it's easier to keep other commitments as well.

Today's action for success:

I like to keep lists. I know that it is a simple writing practice, but it gives me satisfaction and personal freedom. When I write down an item on my to-do list, it holds me accountable and also frees up my mind because I do not have to consciously remember it. I know that it will be there on my list to accomplish in due time. Once a task is complete, it is so liberating to cross it off and even write DONE next to it. Crossing off things on my list gives me an ego boost because I have been responsible and completed a task. Also, more importantly, it allows me to train my soul for bigger and better tasks that the Universe is going to ask me to undertake. Soul training starts small and grows. Nurture your soul through little jobs well done, and then watch out because you will be handed bigger and bigger duties to accomplish that will elevate you spiritually.

SERVICE

Trying to get without first giving is as fruitless
as trying to reap without having sown.
—NAPOLEON HILL

Plant before you can Harvest

The Bible states that we reap what we sow. The most fertile soil in the world is barren unless seeds have been properly planted, cultivated, and nurtured. The relationship between giving and getting is constant in everything you do. To succeed in any endeavor, you must first invest a generous portion of your time and talents if you expect ever to earn a return on your investment. You have to give before you get. It's all a matter of attitude. You may occasionally be disappointed if you are not rewarded for your efforts, but if you demand payment for your services before you render them, you can expect a lifetime of disappointment and frustration. If you cheerfully do your best before asking for any compensation, you can expect a bountiful harvest of the greatest rewards life has to offer.

Today's action for success:

Ever try growing a small garden? If you have, you know that it is not a simple task. Even before the seeds can be planted there is preparatory work to be done. The ground must be prepared to receive the seed. Weeds, brush, litter, and rocks all prevent the soil from being receptive and have to be cleared away. Our minds are like gardens. Thoughts are our seeds. Negative thoughts produce weeds and positive thoughts produce food for action. We cultivate our minds through our experiences in real time and also vicariously. Reading good books allows us to cultivate our minds through the experiences of others, while doing a good deed allows us to fertilize our minds with good, constructive experiences based on our own actions. It has been said that we are the sum total of our thoughts to date. That's an interesting concept when you think that it is also said that "I can read him like a book." Make sure the garden you plant has been enriched and not polluted by your thoughts. And, that your total actions contribute to a book worth reading—maybe even one that is on the *New York Times'* best seller list.

SERVICE

The best recommendation is the one you give yourself by rendering superior service—with the right mental attitude.
—NAPOLEON HILL

Positive Mental Attitude

What others think of you is important, as long as it coincides with what you think of yourself. If you are recognized by others as a positive person who always makes an important contribution, you will be in demand, for there are never enough such people in any organization. Your co-workers will value you, your customers will appreciate you, and your boss will recognize and reward you if you stick with it. You may not become an overnight success, but neither will you fail instantly and permanently. Make it a habit to go the extra mile with a Positive Mental Attitude.

Today's action for success:

What is a positive work ethic? I know of none better than the one an employee displayed for me when asked if he could do the assignment he was given. His simple response to me was: "If it can be done, I can do it." Right then and there, I knew that I had a gem of an employee because his attitude was the right one from the start, and to top it off he had the personal initiative to make it happen. How do you respond to a difficult assignment? Do you tend to think of all the ways it can't be done rather than the ways you can master the task? Human nature causes us to think of the difficulties before we think of the ease in which something can be done. Why not throw your thinking into reverse gear, and say triumphantly that "Yes, I can do it, whatever it is!" And then proceed to figure out how it can be done.

SERVICE

Count that day lost whose descending sun
finds you with no good deeds done.
—NAPOLEON HILL

Good Deed Doer

It is well known among those who make it a practice to help others that doing a service for another benefits the giver as much as—if not more than—the receiver. When you do a good deed for someone else, you become a better person. The positive effect that your good deed has upon you will endure long after it is forgotten by the recipient. Good deeds need not be large or costly. The greatest gifts are gifts of your time and yourself. A kind word or small courtesy will be remembered and appreciated.

Today's action for success:

Thinking about doing a good deed? Is it a monumental one? A save the planet one? A deed that will cause the world to sit up and take notice? Well, well, I bet that deed never becomes actualized because visions of grandeur seldom do. But, what about that little inconsequential deed requiring you to pick up some litter, go out of your way to give someone a lift, pay a compliment to a person who could use one, recognize a talent in someone that may be taken for granted or go unnoticed, or better yet, find a need and fill it. If you adopt this practice, it is always a good way to lull yourself to sleep at night too. Simply recount the good deeds that you have done during the day—for no personal reward—and allow yourself to feel the afterglow, and then peacefully drift off to sleep warmed by these positive remembrances.

SERVICE

Medals and titles will not count when you get to heaven, but you may be looked over carefully for the sort of deeds you have done.
—NAPOLEON HILL

Final Exam

It is a fundamental principle of Christianity, and many other religions, that in the afterlife the only real measure of success will be how you have lived your life, not how much money you have accumulated. Whatever your faith may be, a good rule of everyday behavior is to live your life so that when it is over you can take pride in the knowledge that you have made a difference in the lives of those who have known you.

It's easy in the crush of everyday life to lose sight of the true riches of life, the things that really matter. Psychologist Ilona Tobin defines true success as "giving and receiving love, having physical and mental health, enough wealth to provide you with options, and the time to enjoy them all." Whatever your personal definition of success may be, make sure that it includes a healthy measure of the truly important things in life.

Today's action for success:

What is your personal definition of success? Does it include the mental, emotional, social, physical, and spiritual aspects of who you are? Without a balance in your life you will not be at peace with yourself even if you are successful. Before you write your definition, look at what some others have written. For example, Napoleon Hill states that success is doing whatever it is you want to do in life as long as you do not violate another's rights. This is a good point of departure, but a little vague. Personalize the definition and attune it to your individual preferences and what these choices will look like when you see them manifested in your life. In this manner of forethought, you are creating an image of success that you can walk into as you clarify your vision. Some people call this truth in advance.

SERVICE

The only safe way to boast is by constructive actions.
—NAPOLEON HILL

Talk it Up!

It has been said that it's not boasting if you can really do it. This may be true, but a far more persuasive argument is made when you do it first and talk about it later. Besides, good things that are said about you always carry more weight when they are said by someone other than yourself. When you find yourself tempted to wax eloquent about your achievements, force yourself to pause for a moment, take a deep breath, and ask someone else about their achievements.

Today's action for success:

People who have truly made it focus on others and not on themselves. Why is this so? It's simple to understand. People who have arrived have nothing to prove to others because they are already where they want to be. Now, they define their lives by the good deeds that they do for their fellowmen. It is redundant for them to talk about their success because they have already accomplished their goal. Individuals who are still "wannabees" must continue to put themselves in the position they desire. Picture it this way. Can you imagine Jesus talking to Peter and for the hundredth time telling him about all the great miracles he performed? "Why, Peter, wasn't that my best show? Don't you agree? I can't imagine anyone being able to top that miracle. Can't wait to see what I do next." You get the picture. If you are going to boast, make your boast about someone else and then maybe others will listen to what you have to say.

Success

As I Journey Through Life

I wish to be of service to my fellowmen as I journey through life, and I wish to carry with me, wherever I go, a disposition of sunshine and goodfellowship. To do this I have adopted a guide which I shall endeavor to follow in dealing with my fellow beings throughout life's journey. A part of this guide I adopted in my boyhood days, and a part of it I picked up from observation as I grew into a more mature age and as I learned from personal contact with men and women that life is pretty much what we make it—that we largely control our own destinies and our own progress on this earth. For the benefit of those who may wish to emulate me in adopting so much of my daily guide as may be conveniently put into use by them in their own dealings with their fellowmen. I submit a copy of it as follows:

To train myself so that never, under any circumstances whatever, shall I find fault with a single person, no matter how much I may disagree with him or how inferior his work may seem to be, so long as I know he is sincerely trying to do his best.

To respect my country, my profession, and myself. To be honest and fair with my fellowmen, as I expect them to be honest and fair with me. To be a loyal citizen of the United States of America. To speak of it with praise, and act always as a trustworthy custodian of its good name. To be a man whose name carries weight wherever it goes.

To base my expectations of reward on a solid foundation of service rendered. To be wiling to pay the price of success in honest effort. To look upon my work as an opportunity to be seized with joy and made the most of, and not as a painful drudgery to be reluctantly endured.

To remember that success lies within myself—in my own brain, my own ambition, my own courage, and determination. To expect difficulties and force my way through them.

To turn hard experiences into capital for future struggles. To believe in my proposition heart and soul.

To carry an air of optimism in the presence of those I meet. To dispel ill-temper with cheerfulness, kill doubts with a strong conviction, and reduce native friction with an agreeable personality.

To make a study of my business. To know my profession in every detail. To mix brains with my efforts and use system and method in my work. To find time to do every needful thing by never letting time find me doing nothing.

To hoard days as a miser hoards dollars. To make every hour bring me dividends, increased knowledge or healthful recreation.

To keep my future unmortgaged by debts. To save as well as to earn. To cut out expensive amusements until I can afford them. To steer clear of dissipation and guard my health of body and peace of mind as a most precious stock in trade.

To avoid procrastination in all of its various forms, and never, under any circumstances, to put off until tomorrow any duty which I should perform today.

To endeavor to give something to the world in return for the food and raiment which the world give me, and to so live in the pursuit of my daily occupation that I will make those with whom I come in contact happy.

To reap a rich harvest of happiness from the thought that my aim in life shall be to give happiness, help and encouragement to those around me, and to expect my reward in a generous return of these same virtues, in exact proportion to the seeds I sow which generate them.

Finally, to take a good grip on the joys of life.

To play the game like a man. To fight against nothing so hard as my own weaknesses.

So I may be courteous to men, faithful to friends, true to God—a fragrance in the path I tread.

"As I Journey Through Life"
by Napoleon Hill
Founder of the Betsy Ross Candy Company

1913
From THE FRA
Elbert Hubbard's Magazine.
Elbert Hubbard is the author of *Message to Garcia.*

SUCCESS

Your real courage shows best in the hour of adversity.
—NAPOLEON HILL

Setbacks lead to Success

Some setbacks are so severe that to give in to them means losing the whole ball game. When he assumed command of the Korean War, Gen. Matthew Ridgeway found his forces pushed far to the south, hard pressed by the invaders. Only a determined decision to hold the lines allowed the American forces to keep from being swept into the sea and to eventually regain all the territory they had lost.

When a defeat strikes, you may not have the time to withdraw and contemplate your mistakes without risking further setbacks. Don't succumb to paralysis. It is important to know at that moment what it is you truly desire and to act to preserve your resources and your hope. If you crumble utterly, you will take a blow to your self-esteem that will be hard to repair. Instead, stick to your principles, and you will know, at the very least, that you have protected the most important thing you have. Your successes in life will far outnumber your failures.

Today's action for success:

Think back over your life in increments of seven years. List what major setbacks you have had in each of those periods. Now consider how you have not only survived but thrived because of your unwillingness to surrender. Keeping on when the going gets tough is paramount to ultimate success.

SUCCESS

Before opportunity crowns you with great success,
it usually tests your mettle through adversity.
—NAPOLEON HILL

Clue to Personal Weakness

Adversity provides the resistance necessary to develop the strength to overcome great obstacles. This strength consists of self-confidence, perseverance, and, very importantly, self-knowledge. For if you do encounter a setback, it is a clue to a personal weakness. You may have been hasty in judging a competitor, or you may have been too timid in your vision of what needed to be done. Let adversity be your guide to understanding where you misstepped and which qualities you need to cultivate. No one rejoices in disappointment, but if you are success-conscious, you can turn the situation into a chance for improving your character, an opportunity you otherwise would have missed.

Today's action for success:

Personal weaknesses are hard to confront. Napoleon Hill tells a story about a once wealthy man who became a vagrant, a streetperson and couldn't understand what happened to cause it. Dr. Hill was asked to help this man, but he readily admitted that he couldn't but he knew who could. Marching the man into another room and standing him in front of a ceiling to floor curtain, Dr. Hill informed the ill-kempt man that behind this curtain stood the only man who could help him. Then, the curtain was regally drawn aside to reveal a full length mirror. The man looked at himself squarely in the eyes for a few moments and then left in a rage. However, the story doesn't end here because later that year he returned and thanked Dr. Hill for forcing him to see the truth. He realized that he was both the cause and the cure for his problems. Can you face your man in the mirror?

SUCCESS

The keenest minds are the ones that have been whetted by practical experience.
—NAPOLEON HILL

Theory versus Practice

Theoretical knowledge without practical experience might be compared to a large mass of undirected energy. Until it is focused, it is difficult to direct the energy to a useful end. Practical experience is the lens through which the energy of knowledge may be focused and directed toward activities that will provide the greatest benefit.

When you learn new concepts or have an idea that has not yet been tested, make it a practice to think through its application carefully before implementation. When you have considered the possibilities, and it still seems to be a good idea—get into action. The only way to get practical experience is to get to work executing your idea.

Today's action for success:

Get to the can-do part of your theory called application and thereby put your dreams into practice. It is only through the physical application that your dreams will be manifested in reality. Thoughts are things, but they need a solid foundation on this earth plane in order to reap the hoped for benefits. Castles in the sky remain such until you anchor them to the earth. What castles are floating above you?

SUCCESS

A quick decision usually denotes an alert mind.
—NAPOLEON HILL

Indecision leads to Paralysis

Successful people are decisive. They don't agonize over decisions and thereby miss out on a great opportunity. They gather the relevant information, discuss alternatives with advisers whose opinions they respect, and then make a decision and get on with it. Indecision creates the worse kind of paralysis and, left unattended, can permanently damage you and your organization. If you have trouble making decisions, remember that there are few decisions that are irreversible. If you later discover that you were wrong, correct your course and move on.

Today's action for success:

When you decide not to decide you have made a decision. Ponder this thought and when you realize that just because you believe you are forestalling a decision, you are indeed making one. If opportunities are slipping by you, could it be due to lack of decision making? If so, get started and make some decisions! Don't remain stagnant.

SUCCESS

Know your own mind and you will be as wise as the sages.
—NAPOLEON HILL

Take Charge of Yourself

When you take charge of your mind, you take charge of your life. When you understand your thoughts, feelings, emotions, and desires, you can direct them to any end you choose. Wisdom comes from taking the time to study yourself, to know why you are the person you are.

Taking charge of your mind is a thoughtful, reflective, solitary process. Only you can come to understand the complex inner workings of your own mind, and you must be willing to spend the time and effort that gaining such insight requires.

Today's action for success:

It's good to be in charge. Your self-esteem and personal sense of worthiness are enhanced. You feel purposeful, engaged, and current. Being in charge means you have a direction, a vision, a mission for the future. People look to you and trust you because you have assumed the stance of leadership. Live up to the expectations that you have put forward both for yourself and others. Be enthusiastic and lead others onward to mutual destinations. Take action and go forward! Any dream will do.

SUCCESS

If you know your own mind, you know
enough to keep it always positive.
—NAPOLEON HILL

Know Thyself!

You may not fully understand the complex process that causes electricity to be generated and transmitted to your home. But you understand very well how to apply and use it to illuminate your home, power your computer, and perform hundreds of other essential tasks. The same is true of your mind. No one understands the incredibly complex workings of the brain; we know only that when we use our mind in a certain way, we achieve a desired result. If we think positively, we achieve positive results.

Today's action for success:

Place a drop of black ink into a glass of clear water. Notice how every molecule of water is affected by the small drop of ink. The ink transforms the entire glass of water into something murky and nonpalatable. Likewise negative attitudes color our entire world. They do not reside hidden in one small corner of our person, but pervade our body and our spirit. Question what color you want your essence to be before you let negativity infiltrate your person one negative thought at a time.

SUCCESS

A negative mind never attracts happiness or
material success, but it will attract their opposites.
—NAPOLEON HILL

A Negative plus a Negative never equals a Positive Mental Attitude

You may trick yourself into believing that you are only playing devil's advocate or searching for weaknesses in apparently good ideas, but in the end negative thinking always produces negative results. Just as your mind will work tirelessly to translate your positive thoughts into their physical equivalent, it will work equally hard to create negative results when all of your thoughts are negative.

Today's action for success:

Don't seek out the negative in the positive but rather condition your mind to focus only on the positive aspects of everything. This may seem a little awkward at first, but you always find what you seek. Make certain that you are on a treasure hunt for something good. Look for the God in the good and you will always come out a winner. As you train your body with physical exercise, so too can you train your mind for this type of spiritual marathon.

SUCCESS

Every brain is both a broadcasting station and a receiving station for the vibrations of thought.
—NAPOLEON HILL

Are you Tuned In?

Whatever the actual science of thought transmissions may be, it is true that if you wish to receive the power contained in the thoughts of others, you must condition your mind to receive those ideas. Listening helps condition your mind to receive valuable information contained in the thoughts of others. Set aside any preconceived notions you may have about the topic, and listen attentively and nonjudgmentally to what is being said. Focus on the information, not on the speaker. Try to identify key concepts behind the speaker's words. Train your mind to identify and absorb information that others often miss because their "receivers" are not tuned to the proper frequency.

Today's action for success:

Listen for content and refrain from being judgmental when someone speaks to you. It is said that body language delivers well over 85% of the message, but perhaps that is the reason why messages are so often misinterpreted. Focus on the words being spoken and not the "hidden" message and perhaps better understanding will result. Tone of voice, words in the message, and body language are the component parts of face-to-face communication. Knowing this, analyze how you interpret messages from others and broadcast your own more effectively.

SUCCESS

Your true age is determined by your mental attitude,
not the years you have lived.
—NAPOLEON HILL

Ageless or Aged?

The American clergyman and author Tyrone Edwards said, "Age does not depend upon years, but upon temperament and health. Some men are born old, and some never grow so." No doubt you've known teenagers who were old before their time and seventy-year-olds who had the temperament and enthusiasm of those discovering the wonders of life for the very first time. It is all a matter of attitude.

As you grow and develop, make sure your experience is directed toward the acquisition of wisdom, not the acceptance of cynicism. If you find it difficult to keep an open mind because of previous experiences, remind yourself that you're dealing with different people, that conditions have changed, or that because you are older and wiser, your chances of success are greater than in the past.

Today's action for success:

Invest in a book on growing younger. Read the tips and decide to implement one a week if you are eager or one a month if you have all the time in the world. Only you can change your world. Why not "you then" instead of age?

SUCCESS

You can't control others' acts, but you can control your reaction to their acts, and that is what counts most to you.
—NAPOLEON HILL

Decide not to React

No one can make you feel any negative emotion—fear, anger, or inferiority—without your express permission. There will always be people who find perverse enjoyment in upsetting others, or who simply play upon your emotions so that they can use you for their own selfish purposes. Whether or not they are successful depends entirely upon you and how you react to their negative behaviors.

When you are forced to deal with such people, recognize from the outset that they are trying to upset you, not because of something you may have done to them, but because of some problem they have with themselves. Tell yourself: "This isn't about me. I will not allow this person to upset me. I am in control of my emotions and my life."

Today's action for success:

Feeling a confrontation coming on? Condition your mind for success by deciding in advance not to react. Remove your ego from the situation, and respectfully listen to what the speaker has to say. Respond politely, don't react. And, in conclusion take the communication under advisement. You will not only save face, but you will win the verbal match. This is a good tactic to gain time and step back to consider the best response. Think of it as the pause that refreshes.

SUCCESS

Act on your own initiative, but be prepared
to assume full responsibility for your acts.
—NAPOLEON HILL

Who's Responsible? You are!

One of the primary differences between those who achieve greatness in their lives and those who manage only to "get by" is that successful people learned early in life that they were responsible for their own actions. No other person can make you successful or keep you from achieving your goals.

Taking the initiative means assuming a leadership role, a position that singles you out for praise—and for criticism. The good leader is the one who shares the credit for success with others and assumes full responsibility for failures or temporary setbacks. When you accept responsibility for your actions, you gain the respect of others and are well on the way to creating your own future.

Today's action for success:

Responsibility means that you are the person who reports on time for duty. In the movie, *Men of Honor,* "Cookie" responds to his former sergeant by reporting to the line marked on the floor as commanded. Without his sense of responsibility for the outcome in his life, Carl Brashear would have lived his life out as a handicapped individual incapable of realizing his dream of becoming a master diver. Because he knew only he could report to the line, he changed naval history. Where do you report?

SUCCESS

Constancy of purpose is the first principle of success.
—NAPOLEON HILL

Stay the Course

It is critical to your success that you have a well-thought-out plan for your life and that you stick with it regardless of what others may say and the obstacles you encounter. There will always be faultfinders and those who attempt to persuade you that your goals aren't worth the effort you put into achieving them. Those people will never go far, and they will be the first to ask for your help after you have passed them by. Virtually every successful person has considered giving up at some point in his or her struggle to reach the top. And many breakthroughs occurred soon after those same people rededicated themselves to their purpose. There is no known obstacle that cannot be overcome by a person who has constancy of purpose, a Positive Mental Attitude, and the discipline and willpower to succeed.

Today's action for success:

Napoleon Hill states that only 2% of the entire population operates with a definiteness of purpose. The constancy with which they act is the secret to their success. Without dedication, drive, determination, and action, no destiny would be created. Are you driven by purpose, or do you wander aimlessly from one idea to another? A driven person reaches his purpose because he lets no obstacle stand in his way. This tenacity sees him through. Be single-minded, driven, and purposeful, and you will find the treasure you seek.

SUCCESS

You will never be greater than the
thoughts that dominate your mind.
—NAPOLEON HILL

Think on These Things

If it's true that you become what you think about most, it follows that the quantity and quality of success you achieve in your life will be in direct proportion to the size of your thoughts. If you allow your mind to be dominated by trivial matters, your achievements are likely to be unimportant. Discipline yourself to think about important things. Keep up with what's new in your field and with what's going on in the world. Make a list of good ideas that you can use anytime you are searching for a creative solution to a problem. Remember, small minds think about things; great minds think about ideas.

Today's action for success:

Biblically, we are counseled to think on good things. Dwell on the good, and the good will flow into your life. This has been called the law of attraction, but it takes more than just polarizing our mind for good. It takes action coupled with strength of character to propel ourselves into our best vision of our future self. Think on these things and then act to make them happen.

SUCCESS

Are you waiting for success to arrive,
or are you going out to find where it is hiding?
—NAPOLEON HILL

Seek and Find

The poet John Milton's words "They also serve who only stand and wait" may be both profound and genuine, but the true riches of life are far more likely to accrue to those who actively go out and seek them. Seldom does success come marching in accompanied by a brass band in full regalia. More often, it's achieved by those who labor long and hard.

Take the initiative, and you will create your own opportunities. There is no substitute for action backed up by a well-thought-out plan.

Today's action for success:

Get active. Move. Do something, anything. Stop talking and take the personal initiative to see something through. Whatever it is, the task will demonstrate to you that the outcome is in the doing, so do it now!

SUCCESS

It is always better to imitate a successful man than to envy him.
—NAPOLEON HILL

Imitate rather than Envy

Of all the negative emotions, envy is perhaps the most insidious. It is especially sinister because it destroys you from the inside by replacing all that is positive and productive with negative feelings of anger, jealousy, and despair. But when you congratulate others upon their successes and genuinely wish them well, not only do you give credit to those who deserve it, but you also feel better about yourself. Once you've overcome your envy, you may want to determine what specific actions the other person took to achieve success. Meanwhile, you will have strengthened your relationships by recognizing the achievements of others.

Today's action for success:

Model others for the success that you desire. Be watchful and copy the behaviors of those who are in the position you desire. Following in someone's footsteps is a great compliment to their achievements in life. Emulating others is a learning process. Babies emulate parents, students emulate teachers, and followers emulate leaders. And the world marches onward in the circle of life that leads ultimately to the destiny of the human race. A word of caution, however. Be absolutely certain that the dream you are following is a worthy one. Don't be drawn to things that have momentary worth. Look for the value in the things that have intrinsic worth. The treasure is always within you. You will find it if you look deeply enough.

Wisdom

"I give thanks daily, not for mere riches, but for wisdom with which to recognize, embrace, and properly use the great abundance of riches I now have at my command. I have no enemies because I injure no man for any cause, but I try to benefit all with whom I come in contact, by teaching them the way to enduring riches. I have more material wealth than I need because I am free from greed and covet only the material things I can use while I live."

–NAPOLEON HILL'S PRAYER OF THANKSGIVING

WISDOM

A wise man watches his faults more closely
than his virtues; fools reverse the order.
—NAPOLEON HILL

Nip it in the Bud

We all have within us the potential for greatness or for failure. Both possibilities are an innate part of our character. Whether we reach for the stars or plunge to the depths of despair depends in large measure on how we manage our positive and negative potential. It is doubtful that, if left unchecked, your virtues will rage out of control. Unfortunately, the reverse is not true about your faults. Left unattended, faults have a way of multiplying until they eventually choke out your good qualities. The surest way to control your faults is to attack them the moment they appear.

Today's action for success:

Character is built on virtues. Faults work in reverse. In order to develop our character, it is necessary for a person to concentrate on their good qualities and work consistently to develop these. Although it is not an easy task, by focusing on a virtue a day we can begin the path to self-improvement. It is easy to deny that there is a need, but if we just let happen what happens in our life there will be no progress. To begin this self-work, why not select ten character traits from the life of a person you admire? Read his or her biography to underscore these traits. Next, focus on a trait a day and work to develop it in your character. Traits might include self-discipline, persistence, an attitude of service, kind-heartedness, a willingness to go the extra mile, a desire to live your beliefs, etc. By focusing on the positive and making a commitment in your daily work to enhance one of these characteristics each day, you will be on your way to building a sound character.

WISDOM

Control your own mind, and you may never be controlled by the mind of another.
—NAPOLEON HILL

Mind Control

The mind is the most powerful weapon known to man. It simply cannot be controlled or contained by an outside force, however formidable that force may at first appear. Throughout history, tyrants have tried to control those who opposed them, but eventually these rulers discovered the power of the imagination was far greater than the threat of the sword. As Victor Hugo said, "An invasion of armies can be resisted, but not an idea whose time has come."

Today's action for success:

Consider doing some historical research on the topic of dictators and how their reign ends. Time and time again history demonstrates the strength of the indomitable human spirit. As Dr. V. Frankl tells us in *Man's Search for Meaning*, the last thing we can control when all else is taken away, is our attitude. If our attitude is a positive one, life—no matter how awful—is worth living. Read this book in order to gain a full understanding of the significance of attitude.

WISDOM

The mind serves best which is used most.
—NAPOLEON HILL

Use it or Lose it!

Do you have a continuous improvement program for your most valuable asset—your mind? Make sure that you spend at least a half hour each day studying, thinking, and planning. Review your long-, intermediate-, and short-term goals, and measure your progress to date. Are you on schedule for their completion? Ask yourself, "What information do I not have that would help me achieve my goals?" Then gather the information you need and get into action.

Today's action for success:

Action is the key to success each and every time. Procrastination only helps us dig further into the grave of failure. By writing down your short, intermediate, and long term goals you create a contract with yourself. Reading what you have written reinforces your commitment to your goals. Make it a habit to daily put into writing what it is you want to achieve. As you note your progress, you will become a believer that writing it down makes it happen.

WISDOM

No one has yet discovered the limitations
of the power of his own mind.
—NAPOLEON HILL

No Limit!

Pat Ryan, the chairman and CEO of Aon Corporation, the giant multinational insurance company, is fond of saying, "You can't conceive how high 'up' is, except for the limitations of your own mind." It's not very good English, he admits, but it emphatically makes the point that the only limits that can be placed on the power of your mind will be those you impose on it yourself.

When you brainstorm, don't allow limits to be placed on any idea. Sometimes the ideas that seem the craziest at the time will later prove to be the most inspired. If you're working with your Master Mind group, encourage the free flow of ideas from every individual present. Don't be critical or analytical during the brainstorming process; at this point, every idea is a good one. Cluster the ideas into groups of related thoughts so that the best of them can later be shaped for practical application.

Today's action for success:

Dr. Joe Dudley is CEO for Dudley Products, Inc., located in North Carolina. He tells his life's story in his amazing book *Walking by Faith*. When you read his accomplishments, it is hard to believe that just a little more than forty years ago he started out on his life's mission with a $10.00 Fuller Brush kit. What's more amazing is that he never doubted the power of his own mind. Given his limitations, time and time again he was predicted to be a failure. But, he never accepted another person's opinion of his personal capability. Dr. Dudley knows for certain that the power in his mind is truly without limits.

WISDOM

Sometimes it is wiser to join forces
with opponents than to fight them.
–NAPOLEON HILL

Mutual Advantage

What a better world this would be if we worked together in harmony toward the achievement of our shared goals instead of engaging in petty disputes and turf battles. When you allow yourself to be dragged into personality conflicts, game playing, arguments about who gets the credit, and disagreements about trivial issues, they only drain your energy and sour your attitude. Plus you waste valuable time that could be spent on far more important matters.

When you make an effort to understand others' motivations, you may well discover that your opponents have far more in common with you than you think. When you cage your ego and look at the situation from the other person's point of view, you can almost always find a way to work together for your mutual advantage.

Today's action for success:

Try this today. Go out of your way to do a good deed for someone who least expects it of you. As the wizard in the classic screenplay *The Wizard of Oz* reminds us we should all be good deed doers—or philanthropists in our own right. Sometimes just taking that first step toward doing a kindness will change a perceived enemy into a friend. Why not practice being a daily dispenser of good deeds? If all else fails, it will make you feel better.

WISDOM

No one could ride a horse if the horse discovered its real strength. The same thing is true for people.
—NAPOLEON HILL

Inner Strength

Horses are massive, gentle creatures who are by far larger and stronger than the men and women who handle them, yet they docilely obey the commands they are given. It doesn't seem logical that a large, powerful animal would allow itself to be mastered by a human being, yet we have been able to use our intelligence to dominate the animal kingdom. You can use these same forces to allow the positive side of yourself to dominate the negative. A Positive Mental Attitude allows you to tap the source of great power that resides within you, enabling you to accomplish things you never before believed were possible.

Today's action for success:

Focus on your strengths instead of your weaknesses and sooner than later you will realize the massive power that you can place behind your potential. Living up to our potential is not an easy task because we often are unaware of how to let our "little light shine." One candle can eradicate the darkness, and one deed can begin to put each of us on the path to our definite major purpose in life. Don't assume that you are unworthy. Rather be prepared in advance to call up the majesty that belongs to you and to each of us. Turn your little light into a bonfire and warm yourself by its glow.

WISDOM

Before trying to master others,
be sure you are the master of yourself.
–NAPOLEON HILL

If you can't lead one . . . you can't lead any!

When you develop a Positive Mental Attitude, you immediately set yourself apart from the crowd. You become a leader because positive thinking leads to positive action, while negative thinking leads to apathy and inaction. When you take the initiative in any situation, others will follow simply because they like to associate with people who know where they are going. In order to lead, however, you must first be willing to discipline yourself. The first rule of leadership is never to ask others to do what you are unwilling to do yourself. You can lead only by example. Being a leader requires you to work harder and longer than the others and proving you are the master of your own destiny.

Today's action for success:

Before you can lead, you must follow. Learning the ropes in any organization requires that first you become a good soldier in order to develop into a good leader. Taking orders is sometimes a hard thing to do, but by doing so you are demonstrating your future qualities for leadership. Knowing when to acquiesce and follow command, enables you to assimilate what is going on around you. Seeing life from both the perspective of leader and follower is a good lesson to experience. Really, the best learning is experiential. Never denounce a lesson of value. Rather, grin and bear it. You will be a better person because of the insight you have gained.

WISDOM

Your own mental attitude is your real boss.
—NAPOLEON HILL

Slave or Master?

While your time and your labor may be subject to the demands of your employer and others, your mind is the one thing that cannot be controlled by anyone but you. The thoughts you think, your attitude toward your job, and what you are willing to give in exchange for the compensation you are paid are entirely up to you. It is up to you to determine whether you will be a slave to a negative attitude or the master of a positive one. Your attitude, your only master in life, is entirely within your control. When you control your attitude toward events, you control the eventual implication of those events.

Today's action for success:

When a situation today strikes you as negative, mentally reverse your attitude and focus on the positive in the situation. By forcing yourself to see the good in the bad, the positive in the negative, you are positioning yourself for an attitudinal turn-about. This exercise demonstrates to you that you are always in total control of your outcome. W. Clement Stone always stated—no matter what happened—that God is a good God. This affirmation neutralized the negative and positioned him toward a positive outcome—always.

WISDOM

A mind ill with negative attitudes is more dangerous than a sick body, for its sickness is always contagious.
—NAPOLEON HILL

Mental Illness is Contagious

Experts in human behavior have discovered that it is virtually impossible for an individual member of a group not to be affected by other members. Likewise, the group itself is only as strong as its weakest link. It is rarely possible for the entire group to raise itself to higher levels of achievement than that of which the weakest member is capable. It is only possible for individuals who break out of the group to exceed the potential of the group as a whole.

Don't associate with those who are afflicted with the mental sickness of constant negative thinking. Associate with happy, positive, productive people. Your time is an asset to be managed more carefully than your money; spend it with people who share your desire to succeed and your commitment to maintain a Positive Mental Attitude.

Today's action for success:

A positive mental attitude is the RIGHT mental attitude in all circumstances. Repeat this sentence ten times until it sinks into your subconscious mind. A negative mental attitude services no one. It only spirals one down into the depths of despair. Do not get caught in the maelstrom. Refuse to be negative, and thereby always keep your head above water and yourself afloat.

WISDOM

Keep your mind fixed on what you want in life,
not on what you don't want.
—NAPOLEON HILL

Keep Your Eye on the Goal

We have just begun to explore the inner workings of the mind, but we have long been aware of the effects of our thoughts. When you focus on not missing the target instead of on hitting the bull's-eye, the results are often disastrous, for it is impossible to think negative thoughts in a positive way. Ask any golfer who has tried not to miss a putt or a bowler who has struggled not to miss a strike.

Make sure your goals are specific and precise. "Making a lot of money" or "earning regular promotions" are wishes, not goals. State exactly how much money you expect to earn and when, and the specific promotion you want, how you plan to earn it, and when you expect to do so. As Carlson Companies chairman Curt Carlson once noted, "Obstacles are those frightening things you see when you take your eye off the target."

Today's action for success:

Napoleon Hill's method by which desire for riches can be transmuted into its financial equivalent, consists of six definite, practical steps, viz:

First: fix in your mind the exact amount of money you desire. It is not sufficient merely to say "I want plenty of money." Be definite as to the amount.

Second: determine exactly what you intend to give in return for the money you desire.

Third: establish a definite date when you intend to possess the money you desire.

Fourth: create a definite plan for carrying out your desire, and begin at once, whether you are ready or not, to put this plan into action.

Fifth: write out a clear, concise statement of the amount of money you intend to acquire, name the time limit for its acquisition, state what you intend to give in return for the money, and describe clearly the plan through which you intend to accumulate it.

Sixth: read your written statement aloud, twice daily, once just before retiring at night, and once after arising in the morning. As you read—see and feel and believe yourself already in possession of the money.

WISDOM

Change your mental attitude, and the world
around you will change accordingly.
—NAPOLEON HILL

Make the Change

Your world will become what you choose to make it. You can reach great heights of success, or you can settle for a miserable life that is devoid of hope. The choice is yours. When you choose a positive course, you set in motion an unstoppable force that will allow you to have a fulfilling career, the love of your family and friends, good physical and mental health, and all of the other true riches of life.

To change your world, you must change it from the inside out. You must begin with yourself. When you choose the course that puts your life on a positive track, you will change your life for the better, and you will also positively influence the people with whom you come in contact.

Today's action for success:

Success happens from the inside out. If you want to feel the true glow of success, you must create an inner fire that burns brightly against the dark attitudes of negativity. You must keep the inner fire burning in order to succeed. No one else can do it for you because it will then become their success, not yours. Below are Napoleon Hill's ten personal rules for success:

1. Set your head and heart upon a DEFINITE MAJOR PURPOSE and go to work, right where you stand, to attain it; and begin NOW.

2. Adopt and follow the habit of GOING THE EXTRA MILE by rendering more service and better service than you are paid for, thus enlarging the space you may occupy in the world.

3. Control your MENTAL ATTITUDE and keep it always positive and free from the spirit of defeatism.

4. Apply the GOLDEN RULE in all your human-relationships, no matter what others may do.

5. Learn all that others have discovered in connection with your occupation, job or business, and profit by their experience, thus saving yourself both grief and loss of time.

6. Be prudent with your diet, exercise regularly, and avoid dependence on drugs, alcohol, or tobacco.

7. Keep your dominating thoughts upon the things you desire and demand of life, and off the things you do not desire.

8. Learn to transmute your sex emotion into the attainment of your DEFINITE MAJOR PURPOSE, at will, remembering that this is a creative force of unknown, unlimited possibilities.

9. If you work for another person, do your work HIS WAY, not yours, and do it in a gracious, pleasing manner.

10. Instead of criticizing others (no matter how much they may deserve it) devote your time to the discovery of traits of your own which should be corrected lest they provide the basis of just criticism against you.

WISDOM

Wisdom consists in knowing what not to want
as well as what to want.
—NAPOLEON HILL

Discover Your Talent

Your goals should also be designed to create rewards that are most important to you, not to someone else. Some experimentation may be required, particularly during your early years, to find what you really like and what you're best at. Career and financial goals should be balanced with personal goals such as maintaining relationships with people who are important to you. Your plan for your life should also include some fun goals, doing something simply because you enjoy doing it. Spiritual development is also important in becoming a happy, well-rounded person. Make sure you allow time for all important aspects of your personal development.

Today's action for success:

Make certain that you pursue the following areas of your life to their fullest: spiritual, emotional, social, mental, and physical. Pretend that these are spokes on a wheel. Consider on a scale of 1–10 (10 being the exterior of the wheel) how advanced you are in each area. Draw a wheel with your spokes extending to the length you have indicated for each. Next, connect one spoke to the next and see if your wheel forms a perfect circle in circumference. If not, is it any wonder why your wheel of life doesn't roll too easily? Make the necessary adjustments and get moving!

WISDOM

If you really are smarter than others, show them with your actions.
—NAPOLEON HILL

Action Always Speaks Louder than Words

It is a natural human reaction for you to wish to correct others when you see them making a mistake or doing something differently than you would have done it. It is far more difficult to control the impulse to show them how much more intelligent you are. The ability to recognize and control such impulses marks the beginning of the development of wisdom. A wise person knows that when he shows his intelligence with the actions he takes, others learn a far more valuable and lasting lesson.

If you see someone who could benefit from your advice, you can gently lead him to a more appropriate conclusion by asking open-ended, nonjudgmental questions. Let others find the flaws in their reasoning by leading them logically through the process. As Ralph Waldo Emerson once said, "The secret of education lies in respecting the pupil."

Today's action for success:

Dr. Hill states: "Opinions are the cheapest commodity on earth. Everybody has them." The message in this thought is that people most often mirror what you do rather than what you say. Why waste valuable time talking and giving unheeded advice? Rather, rev up your action motor and travel to a place that is a destination rather than a pit stop. Remember—thought + action = success. As Gandhi states, "Be the change that you want to see in the world."

WISDOM

Good intentions are useless until they are
expressed in appropriate action.
—NAPOLEON HILL

Sin of Omission

Good intentions may be an appropriate starting point for achievement, but they will go nowhere unless you follow through with action. Many people confuse intentions with achievement; after all, it is the idea that is most important, they reason. In reality, the most mediocre idea acted upon is far more valuable than a flash of genius that resides only in your mind. Developing the habit of action may be difficult at first, but the more you practice it, the easier it becomes.

Today's action for success:

Are you guilty of having the greatest of intentions but no follow through? Knowing what you would like to do and doing the action is not the same thing. Refine your thinking and get moving in the direction that you want to take. It is only in the doing that we arrive. Be a completer, a doer, an action oriented person, and because of the steps you take you will immediately perceive the difference in your life. Think of it this way, what happens when a gentleman caller fails to bring candy and flowers to his beloved on Valentine's Day, but states that he had the greatest intention of doing so? It doesn't take too long to forecast the outcome of this relationship if the man's greatest intention doesn't match his action. The proof, as is said, is in the pudding.

WISDOM

Nature yields her most profound secrets to those who are determined to uncover them.
—NAPOLEON HILL

Search for Solutions

The field of science is perhaps the best illustration of how success always seems to come to those who apply the principle of accurate thinking in a persistent, determined effort. America's great inventor Thomas A. Edison is said to have failed 10,000 times in his attempt to develop a workable electric light-bulb. He learned from each failure and refused to quit until he succeeded. Breakthroughs occur every day because a determined person continues to search for solutions to complex problems long after everyone else has given up and gone home. You may not invent the lightbulb or the next supercomputer, but you can find creative solutions to old problems if you apply the proven principles of success consistently and persistently.

Today's action for success:

Persistence is the key. By being persistent a person can surpass others who tire easily and make it to the finish line. It's not about being the best or the brightest, but rather the person who is the most persistent who most often takes home the trophy. Recall times when you displayed persistence and won because you simply refused to give up. Nature seems to delight in those individuals who are too stubborn to be dissuaded from their mission. Take no intermission from your mission, and in the end you will be awarded the coveted prize. Persistence is the key.

Work

We would like to call your attention to the only formula in this philosophy. It is called the $Q^1 + Q^2 + MA = C$ formula because these are the initial letters of the equation:

Quality of service rendered
plus
Quantity of service rendered
plus the
Mental Attitude in which it is rendered
equals—

Your compensation in the world and the amount of space you will occupy in the hearts of your fellowmen.

The word compensation here means all the things that come into your life: money, joy, happiness, harmony in human relations, spiritual enlightenment, peace of mind, a positive mental attitude, the capacity for faith, the ability and desire to share blessings with others, a mind that is open and receptive to truth on all subjects, a sense of tolerance and fair play, and any other praiseworthy attitude or attribute you may seek.

Source: *PMA Science of Success*. The Napoleon Hill Foundation. 1983, pg. 159.

WORK

When you ask another person to do something, it may help both him and you if you tell him what to do, why he should do it, when he should do it, where he should do it, and how he may best do it.

—NAPOLEON HILL

Your Mission if You Accept It

We are all influenced by our background and experience. We perceive instructions in the context of our education, experience, heritage, the culture of our organization, and a number of other variables. Good managers know this, and they make sure that their instructions are clear, concise, and well understood. They also know that they must walk a fine line between conveying adequate instructions and killing workers' incentive by not allowing them sufficient latitude to do their jobs.

You may strike the right balance between instruction and motivation by encouraging employees to participate in setting objectives for themselves and their team, helping them develop a plan for achieving their goals, and by making sure that each individual clearly understands the team's mission and his or her role in achieving it. Suggest that team members check in occasionally to report their progress, then get out of their way and cheer them on to victory.

Today's action for success:

Sit down with those you work with—family, friends, co-workers, etc.—and create a "to-do" list of goals that are clearly stated and understood. Reach a mutual, verbal agreement that these goals are beneficial to all concerned, and then make a game of crossing off one by one until the last goal is reached. Celebrate your completion with a form of recognition for each group member. Pats on the back and hugs are always good means of reinforcement too.

WORK

Isn't it peculiar that some people are so clever at inventing alibis and so dull at doing the job that would make alibis useless?
—NAPOLEON HILL

What's Your Alibi?

If folks did their jobs with half the effort and creativity they waste in vain attempts to deceive others, they could achieve great success at anything. It is tempting at times to emulate those who seemingly get by without working very hard, but those who cheat the company by not doing what they are paid to do will eventually pay the price. They will pay with the loss of their most valuable possession: their reputation. The value of a reputation for honesty and integrity is the difference between a career filled with promise and a life of failure.

Today's action for success:

A good spot check on the alibis you live by can be achieved by creating a list of your goals on the left-hand side of a sheet of paper. List 10 to 20 goals in column fashion. Now, on the right hand side, consider what keeps you from achieving these goals. This is where your alibis will rear their ugly heads. Once you see them for what they are—big drawbacks to your success—you need to eradicate them one by one. Only when you pull them up by their roots will you be rid of them forever.

WORK

If you don't want your life to be "messed up,"
don't fool around with those who have messed up theirs.
—NAPOLEON HILL

Too Close for Comfort

It is a peculiarity of human relationships that it is virtually impossible for one individual to have a lasting positive influence upon members of a group of negative thinkers. Usually, it works the other way. You cannot maintain a positive, productive attitude if you spend all your time with negative people. Those who have wrecked their own lives (and usually blame their misfortune on others) are not the kind of people who will help you achieve success in your own life. Choose your friends and associates carefully, and refrain from complaints about your job, your company, or any individual. Spend your time with positive, ambitious people who have a plan for their lives. You will find that their optimism is infectious.

Today's action for success:

If you are going to catch someone's attitude, it might as well be a good one. When people begin to complain, gossip, and downgrade life in general, take this as your cue to leave the premises. Nothing good is going to show up as long as you are in bad company. Give yourself marching orders and step out of negativity into the positive future that you foresee for yourself. Even if you are traveling alone, it is well worth the trip.

WORK

If life hands you a lemon, don't complain, but instead make lemonade to sell to those who are thirsty from complaining.
—NAPOLEON HILL

Thirsty?

Wally Amos, the man whom many consider to be the father of the gourmet cookie industry, has turned lemons into lemonade so often in his life that in his official portrait he holds a pitcher in one hand and a glass of lemonade in the other. A perennial optimist, Amos refuses to acknowledge that obstacles are anything other than stepping-stones to success. In a career that has spanned several decades, he has made it to the pinnacle of success several times, only to lose everything and be forced to start over. But he's never lost faith. "You have to have the trust and faith to let go and not agonize," he says. "Don't waste your time worrying. Worry is not preparation. Analyze the situation and focus on solutions. There is always an answer."

Today's action for success:

Reflect on things from your life that started out as adversities, but turned into benefits over time. These types of things are hard to recognize close up, but with time and distance, a person is usually able to detect the blessing in the loss. Once this happens our awareness level is raised and the process can be accelerated. Knowing that there is a hidden benefit in all adversities, we can begin to look for the seed of an equivalent benefit when something throws our life into reverse gear. Instead of waiting for time to pass, create your own future by planting your seeds of choice. In this manner, you can plan your garden and reap the harvest ahead of schedule.

WORK

Remember that every time you go the extra mile,
you place someone under obligation to you.
—NAPOLEON HILL

Practice GEM

When you do something to or for another, whether your deeds are good or bad, people feel compelled to "retaliate" in kind. If you are a kind and decent person, you can expect to be treated well in return. If you use others for your own advantage without giving anything in return, you will soon find that they have little use for you. People like working for and with positive, considerate people. Start now to develop the habit of going the extra mile.

Today's action for success:

Do you live to get or to give? Serious question. What motivates you in life? If you are a giver, life will respond in kind and the Universe will be cooperative with your desires. If you are a "getter," your true self will be uncovered. As the Bible states, "It is in giving that we receive." Be a giver and thereby give yourself the ultimate gift that only you can bestow.

WORK

The end of the rainbow is reached
only at the end of the second mile.
—NAPOLEON HILL

Real Treasure!

Christ's admonition to the faithful in Matthew 5:41: "And whosoever shall compel thee to go a mile, go with him twain," was in response to the Roman custom of allowing officers to force others to carry their load for a mile. The purpose of the biblical principle, similar to the idea of turning the other cheek, was to make good come from evil. You can add goodness to goodness by rendering beyond what you are asked to do. When you truly believe that the habit of going the extra mile is the only acceptable way to conduct yourself in all your dealings with others, when you are driven by a burning desire to serve your fellow man, you will be rewarded both financially and personally.

Today's action for success:

An old song goes "give a little to get a little," but the new emphasis is on giving beyond the usual expectation. Do more than is expected, and you will reap more benefits over time. Show up early consistently for work, skip lunch on occasion to complete a project ahead of schedule, give a co-worker a hand without expecting a return favor, look for a need to fill and then fill it, and you will be blessed beyond measure. Look out for the good vibes that will be coming your way from sources known and unknown.

WORK

Start going the extra mile and opportunity will follow you.
—NAPOLEON HILL

Render More and Better Service

Going the extra mile can give you insight and a good reputation, both of which attract opportunity. Many obvious opportunities are found in places no one else has bothered to venture. If you put in the extra effort to make a good project an even better one, or you get to know your equipment better than anyone else on your shift, you will see things others overlook and be in a position to make use of them.

Leaders who need a job done think first of people they know who will do it well. If other people respect you for the quantity and the quality of your work, you will find yourself advancing past others who regard their jobs as drudgery. For all the extra service that you've rendered, you'll find yourself more than amply compensated by opportunities others never grasp.

Today's action for success:

Look for hidden opportunities. See the yin and the yang. If you have a problem, the likelihood is that others have the same problem as well. Finding a solution to the problem will not only enhance your life, but it has the potential to enhance the lives of those who you come into contact with. Be entrepreneurial in your outlook, and you will not only be of service to others but also to yourself.

WORK

Those who do no more than they are paid for
have no real basis for requesting more pay because
they are already getting all they deserve to earn.
—NAPOLEON HILL

Paid in Full

If you look around you, it will be apparent that there are two types of people in the world: There are those who say, "When this company decides to pay me what I'm worth, then I will do what they want me to do." The second is the person who says, "I'm going to be the best I can be because that's the kind of person I am. I also know that if I consistently give more than expected, I will eventually be rewarded for my efforts." It is easy to see that the positive person contributes most to the organization. Yet, very few people are willing to make the sacrifices necessary to achieve success. Make sure you're a member of that group.

Today's action for success:

Does your price tag display your worth? Think about it. Are you really worth the salary you earn, or are you being overpaid? Or maybe underpaid? Only you can answer that question honestly. However, it is always good to know your true worth even if you are underpaid because compensation can be gotten for a job well done in many ways. Ask yourself how you are compensated by your job other than a paycheck. Require yourself to list the additional benefits. Before you know it, you will realize that your salary is only a token of your total worth. As a child of the Universe, you are indeed priceless.

WORK

Some individuals appear to be "allergic" to honest work, but opportunity is equally allergic to them.
—NAPOLEON HILL

Doer or Drifter?

In any business, profession, or occupation, there comes a time when you have to deliver. You may fake it for a time, pretending that you're giving an honest effort, but eventually you will be measured by your deeds, not by your words. If you are more of a talker than a doer, make a vow today—right now—to change your behavior. You may be able to drift through life if you never do more than you are required to do, but you will never know what you might have achieved if you had only been willing to give a little more. The greatest opportunities always go to those who have an affinity for hard work, not an allergy to it.

Today's action for success:

Are you allergic to hard work? Does work cause you to react in a negative way? Do you avoid it like the plague? Are you getting the creepy-crawlies just thinking about work? Well, if those are your symptoms you can rest assured that you can cure yourself of work by not showing up for your life's mission. Just retreat, and accept the defeat that you have chosen for yourself. When you give up work, you give up life. Only you can decide if you will walk away from life's challenges or step up to the plate.

WORK

Do your job precisely as if you were your
own boss, and sooner or later you will be.
—NAPOLEON HILL

Who is your Boss?

The American system of free enterprise is based upon the premise that every individual may profit in proportion to his or her labors. In today's hectic, highly competitive, global environment, however, you may feel that you are not adequately recognized and compensated for the contribution you make. The next time you feel overworked, underpaid, and unappreciated, remind yourself that you really are in business for yourself. Your product is you.

Are you the kind of employee you would like to have if you were the boss? When you are considering a difficult decision or when you are thinking about how to avoid an unpleasant assignment, ask yourself, "If this were my company, how would I handle this situation?" When your answer is that you would take precisely the same action you are considering as an employee, you are headed for bigger and better things. You will soon be the boss.

Today's action for success:

First you practice leading yourself, and then you lead others. You must do the routine many times before you can excel. Practice makes perfect, and persistence is the key. We crawled before we walked, we were read to before we read, we grasped crayons before pens, and we studied before we taught. The logical order to things demands that first we perform and then we perfect. What are you about perfecting?

WORK

When the going is hardest, just keep on keeping on, and you'll get there sooner than someone who finds the going easy.
—NAPOLEON HILL

Keep on Keeping On

If you think achieving great heights of success will be easy, you either don't understand at all how the process works or you have your sights set too low. Reaching the top of any field is difficult, time-consuming, and often tedious. The reason it isn't crowded at the top is that most people won't do the things that are necessary to achieve success. They are all too willing to give up when the going gets tough. If you need inspiration to persevere, read the biographies of men and women who have achieved greatness in their lives. You will find that they prevailed because they refused to quit. They continued to toil alone long after the masses had given up and gone home.

Today's action for success:

Winston Churchill states, "Never give in—never, never, never, never, in nothing great or small, large or petty, never give in except to convictions of honour and good sense. Never yield to force; never yield to the apparently overwhelming might of the enemy." If we just follow this one piece of advice in our chosen field we will be a success 100% of the time. Fact: persistence creates more winners than genius.

WORK

Have you noticed that the most effective worker
is generally the busiest?
—NAPOLEON HILL

Be Busy

Successful people are busy people. They despise idleness and constantly search for new challenges and better ways to do things. When others discover that you are a thoughtful, helpful, enthusiastic worker, you will soon have more business than you can manage, and you will greatly increase the number of people who have a stake in your success.

The most mundane tasks become much more bearable when you compete with yourself to improve at doing them. When you find faster and better ways to do your job, you also free up time that can be spent in more creative pursuits.

Today's action for success:

How can you budget your time and money in order to accelerate your success? Napoleon Hill states that using our leisure time wisely is the key. The eight hours dedicated to leisure time could be put to constructive use. If you use a portion of this time daily to study in an area of your personal interest, research indicates that in three year's time you will be known locally in this field, in five year's time, you will be know nationally, and in seven year's time, you will be known internationally. Seems like a real investment deal!

WORK

The quality and quantity of service you render fixes your wages and determines what sort of experience you are getting.
—NAPOLEON HILL

Quality and Quantity

The only constraints that you have on your income and advancement potential are those you place upon yourself. If you don't like your position, or if you are unhappy with your salary, do something about it. What can you do to make yourself more valuable to your department or your company? What tasks have not been completed because no one has the time or the inclination to take care of them?

Look around and identify things that need to be done. Don't wait to be asked. If you make it a habit to seek out opportunities, to take on new tasks, you will increase your knowledge about the organization and become such a valued employee that your company can't afford to lose you.

Today's action for success:

Make yourself indispensable by becoming a jack of all trades within your organization. Emulate the kindergartner who screams—"I can do it, I can do it!" And, then asks in the next breath, "What is it?" Enthusiasm like this generates fantastic job security.

WORK

The chances are that your job likes you
precisely as much as you like it, but no more.
—NAPOLEON HILL

Love it or Leave it

You are the world's greatest expert on your job, and you can make it into what you choose. You may have a job description, but there are few jobs in the world that come with detailed instructions. A job description simply provides a foundation upon which you may build the perfect job for yourself. When you give generously to it, a job responds with a full measure of satisfaction, personal growth, financial rewards, and promise for the future.

If you are in a job you absolutely hate, and you have considered all the alternatives and decided that you will never like your job, find something else. But if you, like most people, dislike a few things about your work, but on balance believe you have a pretty good position, get busy making it the greatest job in the world. In your career, as in life, you get in direct proportion to what you give.

Today's action for success:

Focus on what you like about your job, and decrease the focus on what you dislike. If you consider what it is about your job that is rewarding, and dwell on these things rather than what you hate, your outlook and next your job will improve. It's easy to fill out a complaint list of "what's wrong with my job." Why not create a praise list for a change about what's right with it? Remember, we increase what we focus on. Do you want to focus on the negative or the positive?

WORK

You must get busy doing something about going the extra mile.
—NAPOLEON HILL

Andrew Carnegie's Favorite Principle—GEM

It's well and good to feel as though you have changed the attitude with which you render extra service, but if that service is in truth no more than anyone else's, then you aren't doing yourself much good. You need to examine your co-workers and competitors to understand just what it is that will make you stand out. If there are job performance standards, exceed them. If you're fulfilling a contract, make sure you offer more than you promised.

You cannot confine extra-mile service to your work alone. You must make it part of your philosophy for dealing with every person you encounter. Imagine how others will be delighted to find that you are the type of person who not only does what is promised but even delivers more. The true benefit of going the extra mile is in teaching yourself to strive always for better and greater achievement in all that you do.

Today's action for success:

Are you a promise keeper, or are you a dream buster? Do you lift people up, or do you pull them down? Are you a negative sounding soothsayer, or a prophetic inspiration? Do you forecast gloom and doom, or are you as bright as Tinkerbell? Which costume do you choose? It's really up to you. Why not dress for success, and color your attitude with a song? Go the extra mile, and even name the street for yourself!

STUDY GUIDE

ACHIEVEMENT

Where will you be ten years from now if you keep on going the way you are going? (1)

Don't be afraid to aim high when choosing your life's goal, for no matter how high you aim, your achievements may fall below it. (2)

A rudderless ship and a purposeless person are eventually stranded on desert sand. (3)

By all means tell the world how good you are—but . . . (4)

Watch the one ahead of you, and you'll learn why he is ahead. Then emulate him. (5)

If you want a job done promptly and well, get a busy person to do it. The idle one knows too many substitutes and shortcuts. (6)

Never mind what others didn't do. It's what you do that counts. (7)

Most misfortunes are the result of misused time. (8)

When you close the door of your mind to negative thoughts, the door of opportunity opens to you. (9)

You are more apt to "rust" out your brain from disuse than you are to wear it out from use. (10)

Some people are never free from troubles, mainly because they keep their minds attuned to worry. The mind attracts what is dwells on. (11)

The best job goes to the one who can get it done without passing the buck or coming back with alibis. (12)

Your progress in life begins in your own mind and ends in the same place. (13)

If you work as hard at the task you desire to do as the task you must do, you will go places. (14)

Remember, your mental limitations are of your own making. (15)

ADVERSITY

Great achievement is born out of struggle. (1)

Don't look to the stars for the cause of your misfortunes. Look to yourself to get better results. (2)

The person who complains that he or she never had a chance probably hasn't the courage to take a chance. (3)

No one can keep you down but yourself. (4)

It isn't defeat, but rather your mental attitude toward it, that whips you. (5)

Who told you it couldn't be done, and what great achievements has he performed that qualified him to set up limitations for you? (6)

If you don't know what you want, don't say you never had a chance. (7)

It's not the epitaph on your tombstone but the record of your deeds that may perpetuate your name after death. (8)

Many successful people have found opportunities in failure and adversity that they could not recognize in more favorable circumstances. (9)

Edison failed 10,000 times before perfecting the incandescent electrical light bulb. Don't worry if you fail once. (10)

Success requires no explanation; failures must be doctored with alibis. (11)

There always remains an opportunity to make a new start. (12)

Most failures could have been converted into successes if someone had held on another minute or made more effort. (13)

Success attracts success and failure attracts failure because of the law of harmonious attraction. (14)

Failure seems to be nature's plan for preparing us for great responsibilities. (15)

COOPERATION

A good football team relies more on harmonious coordination of effort than individual skill. (1)

Friction in machinery costs money. Friction in human relationships impoverishes both the spirit and the bank account. (2)

If you cannot agree with others, you can at least refrain from quarreling with them. (3)

Remember, it takes at least two people to carry on a quarrel. (4)

Friendly cooperation is never any part of the devil's work. He is working on the other side. (5)

All enduring success is founded upon harmonious human relationships. (6)

If you appreciate the kindness shown you by others, say it with actions as well as words. (7)

Willing cooperation produces enduring power, while forced cooperation ends in failure. (8)

No one can succeed and remain successful without the friendly cooperation of others. (9)

Cooperation must start at the head of a department if it is expected at the other end. The same is true for efficiency. (10)

Friendly cooperation always pays off because this sort of teamwork creates a positive mental attitude, which does not recognize obstacles. (11)

Remember that no one can hurt your feelings without your cooperation and willingness. (12)

Try telling your boss about the things you like, and see how willingly he or she will help you get rid of the things you don't like. (13)

Unlimited power may be available when two or more people coordinate their thoughts and actions in a spirit of perfect harmony for the attainment of a definite purpose. (14)

Those who can't take directions graciously have no business giving them. (15)

ENCOURAGEMENT

Making life "easy" for children usually makes life "hard" for them in adulthood. (1)

Most of us don't mind being told of our faults if the critic is generous enough to mix in a few of our virtues as well. (2)

The worst thing about worry is that it attracts a whole flock of relatives. (3)

If you can't manage your own mental attitude, what makes you think you can manage others? (4)

A positive mind finds a way it can be done. A negative mind looks for all the ways it can't be done. (5)

Your mental attitude is the most dependable key to your personality. (6)

Remember that no one is ever rewarded or promoted because of a bad disposition and a negative mental attitude. (7)

Don't look to the stars for the cause of your misfortunes look to yourself to get better results. (8)

Self-respect is the best means of getting the respect of others. (9)

It takes more than a loud voice to gain respect for authority. (10)

It is always safe to talk about others as long as you speak of their good qualities. (11)

Instead of complaining about what you don't like about your job, start commending what you do like and see how quickly it improves. (12)

You can do it if you believe you can. (13)

You come finally to believe anything you tell yourself often enough—even if it is not true. (14)

Might throws itself on the side of those who believe in right. (15)

FAITH

A most beneficial use of time is silent meditation, while searching for guidance from within. (1)

The greatest cure known for loneliness, discouragement, and discontentment is work that produces a healthy sweat. (2)

A negative mind spawns only negative ideas. (3)

It doesn't pay to look at others through a foggy mental attitude. (4)

A positive mental attitude is an irresistible force that knows no such thing as an immovable body. (5)

If you are sure you are right, you need not worry what the world thinks. (6)

Most illness begins with a negative mind. (7)

Individuals with positive mental attitudes are never found in a rut. (8)

If you don't believe it yourself, don't ask anyone else to do so. (9)

If you don't know why you failed, you are no wiser than when you began. (10)

Never tear down anything unless you are prepared to build something better in its place. (11)

Be sure about what you want from life and doubly sure of what you have to give in return. (12)

The value of actions depends on the courage they require. (13)

If you think you can buy your way into heaven with money alone, you may regret that you didn't convert it into good deeds instead. (14)

Faith is a combination of thoughts and actions. (15)

OPPORTUNITY

The man who dipped a chunk of ice cream in chocolate and called it eskimo pie made a fortune for the five seconds of imagination it took to create the idea. (1)

Clarence Saunders made millions by borrowing the self-help cafeteria idea for the grocery business and naming it Piggly Wiggly. Imagination pays! (2)

The imagination is the workshop of the soul, where are shaped all the plans for individual achievement. (3)

Your job will never be any bigger than your imagination makes it. (4)

If you have a better way of doing anything, your idea may be worth a fortune. (5)

The mind grows only through use, and it atrophies through idleness. (6)

Remember the mind grows strong through use. Struggle makes power. (7)

Those who will not take a chance seldom have one thrust upon them. (8)

This is a fine world for the person who knows precisely what he or she expects from life and is busy getting it. (9)

Opportunity has a queer way to stalking the person who can recognize it and is ready to embrace it. (10)

Those who are quick to see their limitations generally are slow in seeing their opportunities. (11)

Don't ever admit that the world has not given you an opportunity. (12)

If it isn't your job to do it, perhaps it is your opportunity. (13)

Opportunity often knocks—only to find no one in. (14)

A resourceful person will always make opportunity fit his or her needs. (15)

SERVICE

The richest persons are those who give most in service to others. (1)

Only the highway of useful service leads to the city of happiness. (2)

When you start giving out, you'll soon begin taking in. (3)

If you have something you don't need, give it to someone who needs it. It will come back to you in one way or another. (4)

The surest way to promote yourself is to help others get ahead. (5)

If you are a shepherd, be the best and you may live to own the flock. (6)

The climb upward will be easier if you take others along with you. (7)

The greatest of all success rules is this: Do unto others as you would if you were the others. (8)

The quality and quantity of the service you render, plus the attitude with which you render it, determine the amount of pay you get and the sort of job you hold. (9)

Dependability is the first foundation stone of good character. (10)

Trying to get without first giving is as fruitless as trying to reap without having sown. (11)

The best recommendation is the one you give yourself by rendering superior service—with the right mental attitude. (12)

Count that day lost whose descending sun finds you with no good deeds done. (13)

Medals and titles will not count when you get to heaven, but you may be looked over carefully for the sort of deeds you have done. (14)

The only safe way to boast is by constructive actions. (15)

SUCCESS

Your real courage shows best in the hour of adversity. (1)

Before opportunity crowns you with great success, it usually tests your mettle through adversity. (2)

The keenest minds are the ones that have been whetted by practical experience. (3)

A quick decision usually denotes an alert mind. (4)

Know your own mind, and you will be as wise as the sages. (5)

If you know your own mind, you know enough to keep it always positive. (6)

A negative mind never attracts happiness or material success, but it will attract their opposites. (7)

Every brain is both a broadcasting station and a receiving station for the vibrations of thought. (8)

Your true age is determined by your mental attitude, not the years you have lived. (9)

You can't control others' acts, but you can control your reaction to their acts, and that is what counts most to you. (10)

Act on your own initiative, but be prepared to assume full responsibility for your acts. (11)

Constancy of purpose is the first principle of success. (12)

You will never be greater than the thoughts that dominate your mind. (13)

Are you waiting for success to arrive, or are you going out to find where it is hiding? (14)

It is always better to imitate a successful man than to envy him. (15)

WISDOM

A wise man watches his faults more closely than his virtues; fools reverse the order. (1)

Control your own mind, and you may never be controlled by the mind of another. (2)

The mind serves best which is used most. (3)

No one has yet discovered the limitations of the power of his own mind. (4)

Sometimes it is wiser to join forces with opponents than to fight them. (5)

No one could ride a horse if the horse discovered its real strength. The same thing is true for people. (6)

Before trying to master others, be sure you are the master of yourself. (7)

Your own mental attitude is your real boss. (8)

A mind ill with negative attitudes is more dangerous than a sick body, for its sickness is always contagious. (9)

Keep your mind fixed on what you want in life, not on what you don't want. (10)

Change your mental attitude, and the world around you will change accordingly. (11)

Wisdom consists in knowing what not to want as well as what to want. (12)

If you really are smarter than others, show them with your actions. (13)

Good intentions are useless until they are expressed in appropriate action. (14)

Nature yields her most profound secrets to those who are determined to uncover them. (15)

WORK

When you ask another person to do something, it may help both him and you if you tell him what to do, why he should do it, when he should do it, where he should do it, and how he may best do it. (1)

Isn't it peculiar that some people are so clever at inventing alibis and so dull at doing the job that would make alibis useless? (2)

If you don't want your life to be "messed up," don't fool around with those who have messed up theirs. (3)

If life hands you a lemon, don't complain, but instead make lemonade to sell to those who are thirsty from complaining. (4)

Remember that every time you go the extra mile, you place someone under obligation to you. (5)

The end of the rainbow is reached only at the end of the second mile. (6)

Start going the extra mile and opportunity will follow you. (7)

Those who do no more than they are paid for have no real basis for requesting more pay because they are already getting all they deserve to earn. (8)

Some individuals appear to be "allergic" to honest work, but opportunity is equally allergic to them. (9)

Do your job precisely as if you were your own boss, and sooner or later you will be. (10)

When the going is hardest, just keep on keeping on, and you'll get there sooner than someone who finds the going easy. (11)

Have you noticed that the most effective worker is generally the busiest? (12)

The quality and quantity of service you render fixes your wages and determines what sort of experience you are getting. (13)

The chances are that your job likes you precisely as much as you like it, but no more. (14)

You must get busy doing something about going the extra mile. (15)

CPSIA information can be obtained
at www.ICGtesting.com
Printed in the USA
LVHW050841070219
606727LV00005B/275/P

9 781722 501112